RELIGIOUS LANGUAGE

RELIGIOUS LANGUAGE

An Empirical Placing
of Theological Phrases

IAN T. RAMSEY

SCM PRESS LTD
BLOOMSBURY STREET LONDON

334 01415 8
FIRST PUBLISHED 1957
FIRST CHEAP EDITION 1967
SECOND IMPRESSION 1969
THIRD IMPRESSION 1973
FOURTH IMPRESSION 1974
© SCM PRESS LTD 1957
PRINTED IN GREAT BRITAIN BY
FLETCHER AND SON LTD
NORWICH

CONTENTS

In this book I hope to show how the concern of contemporary philosophy with language has implications for
theology—its claims and apologetic, its problems and
controversies. I shall argue that, far from being necessarily irreligious, logical empiricism provides us with a
tool which can be of the greatest service to theology,
making possible between philosophy and theology not
only a new co-operation, but a new venture altogether.

Our leading questions must be

(i) *To what kind of situation does religion appeal?*

(ii) *For these situations, what language is appropriate
currency?*

(i) Joseph Butler, in his defence of religion, argued that
(a) we are more than 'gross bodies', and (b) 'probability is
the very guide of life'. These two claims express the
character of religion as (a) an odd discernment, and (b)
a total commitment.

Various illustrations of each of these features.

(ii) Religious language will thus (a) be constructed
from object language which has been given appropriately
strange qualifications, and (b) centre on 'God' as a key-
word which itself becomes the subject of significant tautologies.

No religious apologetic, nor religious teaching will be
worth while if it does not (i) evoke the appropriate kind
of situation and (ii) recommend language of suitably odd
currency.

Chapters II, III and IV give examples to illustrate and
develop this view, and show what implications it has for
religious controversy.

D. *Son of Man*
E. *Miracle Language*

IV CHRISTIAN LANGUAGE:
2. THE LANGUAGE OF CHRISTIAN DOCTRINE

I. The Christian claim is for distinctive situations, and these were originally expressed in a logically riotous mixture of phrases. Christian doctrine begins in an endeavour to systematize these phrases by bringing alongside some dominant idea or model; but qualifiers are always needed to safeguard the Christian claim. In such logical plotting heresy often arises by neglect of logical complexity; the problem of Orthodoxy, however, is to preserve *both* impropriety *and* intelligibility. *Illustrations:* Sonship and Logos; *Theotokos;* hypostatic unity; *Communicatio idiomatum;* Patripassianism.

II. At least three logical areas may be distinguished in Christian doctrine:

(a) *The construction of a revised apex word* (Trinitarian formula) with the traditional Creeds as logical rules for its use.

(b) The attempt to talk of Christian situations in terms of some *relational word* (Justification; Redemption, etc.). Important to be clear about the logical status of such a word; has it 'Key' status? Is it empirically verifiable in terms, e.g., of ethical concepts?

(c) The attempt to talk of Christian situations in terms of *object words* such as 'Church', 'Episcopacy', 'Sacraments', whose various logical placings it is very important to distinguish if unnecessary misunderstandings or confused claims are to be avoided.
Here arise many possibilities of logical blunders and cross-purpose talking. Importance of logical mapping as a preliminary to controversy or doctrinal discussion.

Cydnabyddiaeth a Chyffes

THIS book embodies the substance of four Open Lectures given at University College, Cardiff, under the auspices of Professor Aubrey Johnson. For the most part it illustrates what follows from grounding theological words and phrases in what I have called a characteristically religious situation. To some, a game may itself provide all the reason we need have for accepting its rules; others, less easily satisfied, may ask for an independent and altogether more philosophical discussion of my starting point. These die-hards will, I hope, look sometime in another book which I hope soon to publish under the title of *Fact, Metaphysics and God*. But those points aside, I am sure that there is still much here which could be different and better. The same could not be said, however, of the welcome given to me at Cardiff, or the generous hospitality I received from my friend and former colleague, Dr A. B. Steel, Principal of the College, and Mrs Steel. *Diolch yn fawr.*

I

WHAT KIND OF SITUATIONS ARE RELIGIOUS?

In this small book I hope to show how the contemporary philosophical interest in language, far from being soul-destroying, can be so developed as to provide a novel inroad into the problems and controversies of theology, illuminating its claims and reforming its apologetic. If that seems an astounding suggestion, my hope is that the book will make it less incredible than at first sight it appears.

Let us begin with a brief survey of the historical origins of the contemporary scene. We might perhaps back-date the present philosophical interest in language to the turn of the century when people like G. E. Moore and Bertrand Russell protested against the kind of language being used by the neo-Hegelians who at that time dominated philosophy. To Moore and Russell the language of these neo-Hegelians seemed pretentious, woolly, and confused. There was this talk, for instance, of 'Being' which when 'freely-floating . . . in the air' provided the subject matter of logic.[1] Many of the characteristic claims such as 'time is unreal' seemed to depend on mere juggling with language.[2] Against this, the watchword for Russell, and especially for Moore, was 'clarify'. They would warn us not to think that a philosopher or a theologian is good and impressive because we cannot understand him. What can be said, can be said plainly. If it cannot be said plainly, we should be suspicious of its claim

[1] W. Wallace: *Logic of Hegel: Prolegomena*, p. 302, O.U.P. 1931.
[2] G. E. Moore: *Philosophical Studies*, Lecture VI, pp. 197-219, Kegan Paul, 1922.

to be said at all. It was G. E. Moore rather than C. E. M. Joad, who continually pressed the question 'What do you mean by so-and-so?' and if asked a question himself would answer: 'It depends on what you mean . . .'

As the interest in clarification developed, emphasis came to be centred on the Verification Principle which came to these islands by way of Austria, and is associated with names like Carnap, Schlick and Wittgenstein. This 'Principle' claims, we might say, to give a touchstone for clear and unambiguous language. According to the 'Verification Principle' we must exclude from language all propositions which cannot, at any rate in principle, be verified by sense experience—by what is seen, heard, touched, tasted and smelt. Restrict ourselves to propositions of sense experience and all will be well. Unfortunately, as it seemed to some, not much of language is then left, and in particular ethics and theology would have to be excluded from meaningful language in so far as they claimed to be about anything more than sense-objects. The greatest popularizer in this country of such a 'positivist' view was A. J. Ayer, and his book, *Language, Truth and Logic,* published some twenty years ago, is a landmark in the development of contemporary empiricism.[1]

Now it seemed extraordinary to have to exclude a vast area of language from what could be admitted as meaningful and significant; and even odder that people still continued to use 'meaningless' jargon. More pointedly, what of the Verification Principle itself? It must have an odd enough status, for as presupposed by all meaningful sentences it cannot itself be meaningful in the same sense. So there arose a mellowing of the verificationist outlook, though it is only fair to say that Wittgenstein himself has never shared the

---

[1] It ought to be remembered, however, that Ayer has by now somewhat modified the extreme views which *Language, Truth and Logic* expressed.

more extreme views of some verificationists. There was not only a certain mystical side to his nature; he wanted nothing too cut-and-dried, too technical or precise. We might say however that the mellowing came with the realization that the Verification Principle may only be *one* clue to meaning, so that propositions, however odd by verificationist tests, may yet have a meaning of their own. In other words the view arises that apparently homogeneous language may exhibit all kinds of logical differences.

Here we have the third stage in the development of recent thought: logical empiricism. But let us not think that the mellowing of the verificationist outlook means that the challenge of contemporary philosophy is weakened. It is, in fact, all the stronger for being the more subtle. The third stage has in its turn led naturally to a denial of the possibility of metaphysics, and in this way. If it is the case that language can exhibit all kinds of logical differences, may not all so-called ultimate problems arise from confounding these logical differences and in this way misusing words? Confound logical differences and you will have *pseudo-problems*. 'The Army', we are told, 'marches on its stomach.' If we suppose this is a straightforward assertion, we shall then ask: What kind of animal can the Army be? Is it some kind of cross between a snake and a dachshund? Is it some special kind of Being? So puzzles develop from a misallocation of the original assertion. Or again, confound logical differences and we will have *pseudo-theories* such as the typically scientific claim that 'My table is really only electrons and space . . .', a pseudo-theory which arises from confounding the languages of commonsense and physics. When we come to 'God' we find that believers wish on the one hand to claim that he is indescribable and ineffable, and yet on the other hand to talk a great deal about him. Nay more, when they speak of God they say that he is transcendent and immanent, impassible yet loving, and so on. But if we speak like this, are we talking significantly at all? Here is the Falsification Problem: What kind of talk can this talk about God be, if it permits us to use such conflicting descriptions of God and to continue to use these descriptions in the face of any and all empirical phenomena?

Now it is true that philosophers do not claim as vigorously as they might have done even five years ago, that all the ultimate problems of metaphysics have been created by confounding logics; that these ultimate problems are just category blunders. Nevertheless it is plain that contemporary philosophy lays on us an urgent task and duty, viz. to elucidate the logic of theological assertions, and this book may be seen as an endeavour to face and to measure something of the challenge of contemporary philosophy; to state a case for religious language; to try to elucidate the logic of some of its characteristic claims. Nor is that all. As my first paragraph suggested, I hope to be able to show at the same time the considerable benefits for theological apologetic and controversy which can arise from facing this challenge with which contemporary philosophy presents us. How then do we face the challenge? The answer is, by asking at the outset, and as a leading question: To what kind of situation does religion appeal? What kind of empirical anchorage have theological words?

To answer that question, let our memories first go back to Joseph Butler who in the eighteenth century and in his own way likewise attempted Christian apologetic in the face of contemporary empiricism. If we take up again *The Analogy of Religion Natural and Revealed to the Constitution and Course of Nature*, we shall find Butler makes two points of special interest for our present purpose.

The argument of the *Analogy* is introduced by a discussion in the first chapter of Part I on Immortality. Now I do not think we give this discussion its full significance if we see it as merely meant to establish in a general sort of way the

14

'credibility of a future life'. Rather let us recall Butler's summary of the chapter in his conclusion at the end of Part I. It is, he says there, 'contrary to experience' to suppose that 'gross bodies' are ourselves. Belief in immortality is thus founded in an awareness that as 'living agents' we are more than our public behaviour. Here, I suggest, is the discernment without which no distinctive theology will ever be possible; a 'self-awareness' that is more than 'body awareness' and not exhausted by spatio-temporal 'objects'. Such a discernment lies at the basis of religion, whose characteristic claim is that there are situations which are spatio-temporal and more. Without such 'depth'; without this which is 'unseen', no religion will be possible; though of course for a developed theology much else needs to be said. But here is the bridge-head, the base, call it what we will. And here it seems to me is the abiding significance of Butler's opening Part I of his *Analogy* with a discussion 'Of a Future Life'. We cannot usefully begin theological apologetic without first making plain the distinctive kind of discernment in which theology is founded.

But more needs to be said about this characteristic situation than has so far been covered by calling it a 'discernment', and this brings us to the second memorable theme of the *Analogy*, and one which Butler discussed in an Introduction even before his discussion 'Of a Future Life'. This is the theme which is embodied in Butler's famous phrase that 'probability is the very guide of life'. Now, it is important for us not to misunderstand what Butler had in mind by these words. He did *not* just mean: let us realize how little we know for certain about anything: that doubt and uncertainty pervade knowledge through and through; and so let us be content with a theology which is likewise no more than 'probable'. Let us be content with believing that God probably exists, just as we might say that there probably exists a Dalai Lama. What Butler would say was something very different from, indeed something almost precisely the opposite of, such a half-hearted belief, whose profession makes little or no difference to our lives.

We shall see his point better by first recalling his own words and then giving two examples by way of illustration. 'In questions of difficulty', says Butler, 'where more satisfactory evidence cannot be had, or is not seen; if the result of examination be, that there appears upon the whole, any . . . presumption on one side, and none on the other, or a greater presumption on one side, though in the lowest degree greater; *this determines the question,* even in matters of speculation; and *in matters of practice, will lay us under an absolute and formal obligation,* in point of prudence and of interest, to act upon that presumption or low probability, though it be so low as to leave the mind in very great doubt which is the truth. . . . Nay further, *in questions of great consequence,* a reasonable man will think it concerns him to remark lower probabilities and presumptions than these; such as amount to no more than showing one side of a question to be as supposable or credible as the other: nay, such as but amount to much less even than this. For numberless instances might be mentioned respecting the common pursuits of life, where *a man would be thought, in a literal sense, distracted, who would not act, and with great application too, not only upon an even chance, but upon much less, and where the probability or chance was greatly against his succeeding.*'[1]

Let us illustrate Butler's point by two examples. A man who can scarcely swim is walking by a river. A child, a great distance from the bank, is in difficulties and apparently sinking. Because of the current of the river and his own capabilities, the probability of rescue is very slight. But even though his chance of effecting a rescue might be the slightest possible, we should expect him to jump in (says Butler) with

[1] *The Analogy of Religion Natural and Revealed to the Constitution and Course of Nature.* Introduction: Section 4, ed. J. H. Bernard. The Works of Bishop Butler, Vol. II. (Italics mine.)

the same determination as if he were jumping in on a theoretical background of the highest certainty. 'A man would be thought in a literal sense distracted who would not act and with great application . . .' even when 'the probability or chance was greatly against his succeeding'. Why should we think that the man was 'distracted' if he failed to jump in? Because, Butler says, here is a question 'of great consequence'. The life of a child is something we would die for. Here is a dominating loyalty linked with a world view, and in particular with a certain assessment of personality. If, for instance, we took a different world view—reckoning that the child was only one of millions which nature threw up in an inexorable process of reproduction, so that at best the child was no more than a piece of flotsam with certain possibilities—there would then be no question 'of great consequence' and it would now be unreasonable for the man as a poor swimmer to jump into the river to try to effect a rescue; like all flotsam the child might be left to sink.

Or take another example. We are climbing with someone we love, who slips to fall on a ledge hundreds of feet below. Though we happen to be an indifferent climber, we try to effect a rescue; our whole life is centred to this end. 'I shall make the attempt if it kills me', we would say. 'The probability or chance' may be greatly against our succeeding, but we should be 'thought in a literal sense distracted' if we refused to descend to the ledge because we had not worked out an absolutely convincing theoretical background which would make the attempt cut and dried. The risk we would take is a measure of the 'devotion' which 'inspires' us.

Now it is such a total commitment, appropriate to a 'question of great consequence', a commitment which is based upon but goes beyond rational considerations which are 'matters of speculation'; a commitment which sees in a situation all that the understanding can give us and more; a commitment which is exemplified by conscientious action building on 'probabilities', which Butler thinks to be characteristic of a religious attitude.

So taking Part I of the *Analogy* along with the Introduction, Butler suggests that religion claims (a) a fuller discernment, to which we respond with (b) a total commitment. Such a commitment without any discernment whatever is bigotry and idolatry; to have the discernment without an appropriate commitment is the worst of all religious vices. It is insincerity and hypocrisy.

If then we are to meet squarely the challenge of contemporary philosophy; if we are to make clearer to the unbeliever the kind of empirical anchorage which theological words possess; if we are to enliven apologetic, our first task will be to make clearer what is meant by speaking of situations in terms of 'discernment' and 'commitment'. To do this I suggest that we ask ourselves whether we can find other situations in ordinary life reminiscent of these to which religion appeals? Can we find any parallels from ordinary experience to the two-fold characterization of religion as a discernment-commitment? I think we can, and what I do now is to give some of the examples that come to mind as likely to provide useful parallels.

My first group of examples will, for the most part, illustrate that characteristic of the religious attitude which we have called 'discernment', though even these may also hint at the commitment which the religious man gives to what he discerns. But we shall try to illustrate this commitment more particularly in the second group of examples, though in their turn they may also do something to illuminate the claim for discernment as well. What we are trying to do then in all the examples, is to make it plainer what we mean by calling the religious attitude a discernment-commitment. We must realize from the beginning that no example will tell the full story. But it is our hope that all the examples, taken together, will make much clearer the kind of empirical situation to which theology appeals, will make much clearer to an unbeliever what a religious man is talking about.

A. The first group of situations, illustrating in the main what we have called 'religious discernment' are those about which and not surprisingly, we use phrases that are in certain ways odd, peculiar and unusual. We should say, for instance, of these situations at the point where they provide parallels to religious discernment, that they 'come alive'; that the 'light dawns'; that the 'ice breaks'; that the 'penny drops', and so on.

For our first example let us recall the setting of a High Court—all very impersonal, all very formal, quite lacking in 'depth' and 'vision'. The name of the judge is made as suitably abstract as possible—Mr Justice Brown. The wigs and scarlet are meant to conceal the fact that Mr Justice Brown is after all a human being. If he has rushed to the Court from riding, or mending the car, he would never think of appearing there in riding breeches or overalls. Whatever clothes he wore to play with the children will at least be covered with scarlet and ermine. Nor is the argument of the Court interested in persons. We have, instead, 'the Crown', 'the accused' and 'the prosecution'. Here is a situation as impersonal as may be; a mere façade of human existence. Then, one morning, Mr Justice Brown enters the Court to see as the 'accused' the closest friend of his undergraduate days; or, if we may be more melodramatic, his long-lost wife. 'Eye meets eye'; astonishment; an odd word is uttered. It may be from the undergraduate friend 'Sammy!'; from the wife 'Penny!', and the result is (as the papers will tell us next day) that the Court is 'electrified'. An impersonal situation has 'come alive'. Mr Justice Brown has seen in the 'accused' something he has never seen before, and the accused has seen in the judge of the Queen's Bench Division, something which scarlet and ermine did not express, something which goes far beyond the wigs and the legal language. 'Eye meets eye', but if this phrase is used of the new situation it means far more than physiological positioning; and it is important to see that the significance of words like 'Sammy' and 'Penny' is proportionate to their comparative lack of empirical relevance. The situation has not 'come alive' merely by containing an unusually large range of facts; rather, in stretching to include these facts, the situation has taken on 'depth' as well—it has become in a certain way partly elusive. The very lack of observational ties which nicknames like 'Penny' and 'Sammy' possess, enables them all the better to claim a measure of spatio-temporal elusiveness about the situation of which they are appropriately used. 'Sammy', for instance, may have been a word which, for some quite trivial reason, was associated once with Mr Justice Brown—there may have been some pun on a Sam Browne belt—but it is not used with any observational unpacking in mind, its significance is that it has always belonged to *characteristically personal situations*. 'Penny' may likewise have the thinnest empirical anchorage. Perhaps Mr Justice Brown found a penny by the first stile which he and his wife crossed on the first day of their honeymoon, and with that beginning the word 'Penny' has now come to be currency between them for all that which is most *characteristically personal*. At any rate my point now is that such words would be in violent contrast to the language used normally in the setting of the High Court, and that this violent contrast makes the point (or so I hope) that a characteristically personal situation cannot be contained or expressed in legal language and customs, as it cannot be contained in any 'impersonal' object language. The situation is more than 'what's seen', it has taken on 'depth'; there is something akin to religious 'insight', 'discernment', 'vision'.

Our second example begins with a party all stiff and

formal. Then, it happens that someone's dinner jacket splits unexpectedly up the back; or someone sits sedately on a chair which collapses beneath her. At once the party takes on 'human warmth'; as we should say, 'the ice breaks'. Some theologians who were present might say the party had now entered a 'new dimension'. Once again let us notice that evoking the characteristically different situation is something odd—unusual—though this time it is not odd words but other odd, unusual symbols, like the torn jacket and the broken chair.

For a third example, let us recall the experience we have all had of an argument or a joke in relation to which there is no sort of mutual understanding. We say—and significantly—'I might just as well be talking to a brick wall.' The situation is indeed, as the phrase suggests, impersonal.

But there is one way of assured success, and this will be found if (as we say) we know the weak points in his armour—and once again notice that his personality is concealed by this impersonal word 'armour'. It may be that he is never, as we should say, 'more himself' than when he is fishing. Fishing moves him to tears, reaches the 'roots' of his personality. Nothing so good as a river and fish for evoking 'depth'; fishing is an 'inspiration' to him. Let us suppose then that we are trying to argue the merits of 'equal pay for equal work'. We illustrate it from this angle and from that, but there is no penetration. The head always shakes, and the face looks blank. And then we remember the fishing and we say, 'Look here, Jim, what I mean is "equal fishing pay for equal fishing work",' and he smiles; his face breaks significantly, the penny drops. He says: 'Now I understand perfectly.' Once again it is a word odd to the context which has evoked that characteristically-different situation, which in this case occurs when an argument is grasped, and we 'see' the conclusion in a way which is more than merely 'entertaining' the appropriate proposition.

Incidentally we now have a glimpse of the logical grounds on which swearing has been condemned by religious people. For it is plain that in the story just told, the word 'fishing' could have been replaced by an oath, e.g. 'bloody'. In fact there is a version of the story which does just this and which for reasons of delicacy I avoided. Now it is in situations of high frustration when nothing seems to yield; when a man realizes his powerlessness or finitude; when he is caught up in an entanglement of relationships, that he may be heard to swear. In such words are his cosmic protest, his label for this situation where in some way his existence is shown in its 'authentic' character; when he sees the 'existential' claim of his life; when he knows what 'being-in-a-situation' is. Swearing expresses 'heroic defiance'; it is an assertion of a man's 'being *pour soi*' and so on. So swearing is rightly condemned by religious people because the logic of swearing is so very close to the logic of God. Both appeal to a characteristic situation of discernment and depth, but when a man swears, 'God' is replaced by a word which, even if it is the same token word—made up of the same letters or sounding identical—has no logical connection with a theistic scheme. Swearing is rightly condemned when, in a situation of discernment, an oath takes the place of 'God'.

It will already be clear from this example that the discernment we have in mind as characterizing a religious situation, can be paralleled with those features of particular situations which existentialists refer to when they stress the significance of 'authentic existence' in contrast to merely 'existing'; or again, when they speak of 'being-in-a-situation' or 'participation', or 'involvement', in contrast to being merely a detached 'object', 'spectator' and so on. Situations of religious discernment can be paralleled with those the existentialist wishes to evoke by using such contrasting phrases as these. The religious empiricist will certainly number among his parallels all those situations which

22

existentialists become excited about. Nor will it have escaped the reader's attention that there is an obvious lack of empirical relevance, some strange oddness about the phrases that existentialists use to refer to those situations which they believe to be especially significant. This is sometimes expressed by saying that, for the existentialist, such words as 'authentic' or 'existentialist' are mere catch-words or clichés; but the substance of this criticism is that such typical words tell us very little in a straightforward fashion. In this respect (and we shall take up the point later) they may however be compared with mathematical operators which themselves 'mean' nothing, but are directives of procedure if we want to discover what the mathematical writer has in store for us. So likewise the typical words of the existentialist. Somehow or other they are meant to direct us to the kind of situation the existentialist has in mind, and if they are very often unsuccessful, this should be a warning to the theologian rather than a cause for his criticism. At any rate, the oddness of such words as 'authentic', 'existential', when they refer to situations which can be paralleled with those we would call characteristically religious, is implied by the inverted commas which surround them. These inverted commas have then the same logical status as the hyphens in the other phrase: 'being-in-a-situation'.

The discernment which we have so far tried to parallel by recalling situations where, as it would be said, 'the penny drops', 'the ice breaks'—situations which 'come alive'—this discernment can also be illustrated I believe by the use of such diagrams as are commonplace in Gestalt psychology.

Let us recall how there could be drawn twelve straight lines which at first sight might look no more than two squares with corners joined. But then there dawns on us 'depth', and we see the twelve straight lines as a 'unity'. The lines indeed represent a cube and this cube may, as is well known, seem to enter into or stand out of the surface on which the lines

23

are drawn. Here again is a characteristically-different situation which dawns on us at some recognizable point. This is the point where twelve straight lines cease to be merely twelve straight lines, when a characteristically-different situation is evoked which needs odd words like 'depth' and 'unity', or mathematically the idea of a 'new dimension', 'volume' besides 'area'.

Or again, there is the bread on sale in French shops. We have bread like ∽
bread like ⌒⊃ and o o
and bread like ◯
but if we have been superimposing these shapes in telling the story, we shall then finish not with bread in a shop, but with a Frenchman:
There is a disclosure: the 'penny drops'. ☺

Meanwhile, let me remark in parenthesis that by giving Gestalt examples to afford a parallel to situations of religious discernment, I am not implying that religion is 'purely subjective' or a mere matter for psychology. I do not know what a 'purely subjective' experience is—all experience is *of* something; and as for psychology—certainly all religious situations may be said to be a matter for psychology since they are obviously owned by and experienced by religious men. But that is as true as it is trivial and unimportant. Certainly I am appealing to situations of which we may all become aware. But that does not make them 'subjective', and far from being a theological liability, I should have thought it was an asset, for theological apologetic to be able to make some sort of empirical appeal.

It may, however, be said that these comments avoid the main criticism, which is that such situations as I have given contain nothing which could not be treated in psychological terms and that the Gestalt examples particularly show this to be the case.

Now this challenge is ambiguous:

24

1. It may be implied that all the situations that I have given contain no more than the kind of 'data' for which the techniques and treatment of *experimental* psychology are entirely adequate. In short, it may be suggested that all the situations I have given could be reduced to 'observables' of one kind and another. If so, that is a claim I would strongly challenge. I am well aware, of course, that I have said nothing in this book to *prove* that the situations evoked contain more than 'what's seen'. Whether this could ever be 'proved', or what kind of considerations one would give by way of 'proof' are points which, for our present purpose, I have admittedly set on one side, hoping to treat them elsewhere at a later date. But it can be said at once that the psychological claim no more than mine is established by being asserted, and meanwhile I proceed unabashed and in the confident conviction that any assertion claiming a universal reduction of *all* odd situations to psychological terms, will never be convincingly established. My immediate confidence comes from recognizing what a comprehensive and all-inclusive claim this is.

2. On the other hand, it may be claimed that such situations as we have mentioned could be treated in psychological terms—meaning that they could be treated in terms of some kind of philosophical psychology which, while it builds on, would go much beyond 'psychological data'. This of course would be a more serious challenge. But I would meet it by saying that the challenge is only serious because it more or less meets us on common ground, in so far as it would imply situations not restricted to 'observables'. For this philosophical psychology would now include terms such as 'unity' which I would argue were of metaphysical status; philosophical psychology would indeed be a brand of metaphysics. Once again, however, I am not discussing in this book what makes one metaphysics better than another. I am not discussing how we would justifiably prefer one mapping of a

religious situation to any rival portrayal. I am simply saying:

(a) that here is the kind of situation for which religious language is currency. Religious language is no set of labels for a group of hard, objective 'facts' glanced at by passive observers;

(b) that when theological phrases—whether of a general kind or more specifically Christian—are seen as sponsoring such a situation, they can then be given such a logical structure as by-passes many traditional confusions and controversies which are in fact from this standpoint mere brawling. But I must take this digression no further, and now return to continue our examples.

There are 'disclosures' similar to those we have mentioned, when, for example, we are told someone's name. We may previously have known all kinds of facts about him. We may have had a very great deal of what Russell would have called 'knowledge by description'. We may first have known him as the man in the bowler hat who came to sit next to us in the train. He then appears opposite us at lunch, and we begin to see him regularly. We now know him as the man who invariably orders 'Double Diamond'; the man who does the *Times* crossword in fifteen minutes; and as the weeks pass we come to know him as the man who has a wife and three children; too much herbaceous border to weed in the evenings, too few vegetables left after the frost, too little money left at the end of the month. But one day he says, offering his hand: 'Look here—I'm Nigel Short.' At that moment there is a 'disclosure', an individual becomes a 'person', the ice does not continue to melt, it *breaks*. We have not discovered just one more fact to be added to those we have been collecting day by day. There has now been some significant 'encounter', which is not just a moving of palm on palm, no mere correlation of mouth noises, not just heads nodding in some kind of mutual harmony. The little labels at Conferences do not

26

merely give ostensive definitions of the people behind them; nor do they provoke conversation simply because they associate those people with a background we already know. Not for nothing do people say that the labels 'break the ice' —evoke 'depth', break down the impersonality.

The same kind of 'disclosure' occurs when hills or buildings are named. Suppose we are on a railway or car journey. The countryside might look very much like anywhere else: hills, houses, churches and so on. But then someone has a map or a guide: 'There's Winter Hill', 'That's the Manor House', 'Here is St Lawrence's Church—going back to Saxon times'. Is it no more than additional information? Do we delight to know these details simply because we want to know more facts? Or is it that, with such details, our surroundings become familiar, that this familiarity develops into a feeling of friendship which finally evokes a sense of cosmic kinship where before there were only unknown objects. We not only see the hills, houses, churches, around us, but the landscape 'comes alive'. May not the use of maps and guide books, then, witness to the occurrence of situations parallel to those in which religion is founded?

This first group of examples could plainly continue much further, but I think they will have given some kind of indication of what is meant when religious people talk of an odd 'discernment' and a 'characteristically different' situation. Let no one condemn the examples I have given on the grounds that they assimilate religion to psychology. Let me repeat that the examples are certainly psychological in so far as they appeal to situations which are experienced, but they are *not* psychological in so far as they would reduce religion to what would be called 'subjective experiences'—whatever that phrase may mean. There is no question of a characteristically religious situation being merely 'emotional', if that word is thought to claim that the characteristic features we have been mentioning are entirely (in some sense or other) 'subjective'. Let us emphasize, without any possibility of mis-understanding, that all these situations, all these charac-teristically different situations, when they occur, have an *objective* reference and are, as all situations, *subject-object* in structure. When situations 'come alive', or the 'ice breaks', there is objective 'depth' in these situations along with and alongside any subjective changes.

B. We now turn to our second group of examples which—developing the first—illustrate not so much an odd discern-ment, as the total *commitment* which, along with an odd discernment, makes up what we have claimed to be a characteristically religious situation.

Consider first the kind of situation which people call 'exercising free will'. This is a good example with which to begin our second group because it links closely both discern-ment and commitment features such as those which charac-terize a religious situation. First, the discernment. Let us start by recalling Butler's claim that we have an awareness that we are more than 'gross bodies', more (we might say) than our public behaviour, no matter how comprehensive a view is taken of such behaviour. When we speak of 'exer-cising free will' we likewise claim that there is a situation not exhausted by any tale, however comprehensive, of bodily behaviour; not exhausted by the scientific language of deter-minism, be this ever so complex—involving biochemistry, physiology, psychology, economics and the rest. Of course there are always, those who will assert that all situations called 'exercising free will' are, despite appearances, never-theless tractable in scientific language, for is there not the Unconscious, which is a never-failing hat out of which the determinist can bring impressive rabbits to develop the causal story as far as he wishes? At the moment, however, we are not interested in this particular move, any more than we are concerned with some particular philosophical account of 'free-will' or with adjudging between conflicting accounts. All that concerns us now is that the situation called 'exercising free will', is *prima facie* a particular case of what we have called 'discernment', of a situation which has 'depth'. The claim of 'free will' is that there are occasions of human activity which will not be exhaustively unpacked in scientific language, however far those languages go.

So far, as will be evident, we have not gone beyond our first group of examples, but there is now a further feature of this particular 'free will' situation which we must note. With this discernment there now goes a personal commitment; something which can be seen in the contrasts between choosing to do X, and being told off to do X; deciding to do Y, and being ordered to do Y. We all know the difference, e.g. between choosing to go on a committee and being compelled to do so. There are occasions of course, and those versed in committee politics know the game well, when it is prudent to appear as if one were being compelled to sit on a committee. But no matter what the appearances, and no matter what the psycho-analyst might tell us, it would always be *logically* possible, in answer to someone who said: 'I hear that you were compelled to go on that committee', to retort, 'Not at all; I decided to go on of my own free will'; and if this answer were justified its author would be said to have exhibited (note the adjectives), 'inspired', 'statesmanlike' moves.

Now in all these situations of choosing and deciding, in contrast to being told off or being ordered, there is some possibility, some prospective situation on which our discernment focuses, which we discern as having a claim on us. We 'exercise free will', when we respond to this claim with a response which involves our whole personality. Here then, in 'free will' is the kind of discernment-commitment which we have argued is a feature of a religious life.

Our second example may be regarded as a special case of

the first. The discernment and total commitment which characterize religion, can be illustrated by that pledging of ourselves which occurs when we 'act from a sense of duty'. We need only mention again the illustration from Butler which we have already given.[1] Butler's constant theme is to emphasize that the commitment of religion which arises in relation to its peculiar discernment, resembles very much that personal commitment arising from 'moral' discernment, which characterizes 'conscientious' action.

Further, it is worth noting that Kant, for instance, went one stage further than Butler; for Kant, the discernment-response which characterizes morality is *identical* with that which defines religion. For Kant, a man was 'free' when he discerned a 'moral law' which 'obliged' him, he was 'free' when he was 'obliged' by the moral law. The whole of a man's life, thought Kant, could centre around, and focus on, the discernment and response which the phrase 'moral law' evokes. For Kant the moral law thus defined a total commitment; it was, we may fairly say, the key idea for Kant's metaphysics. But this was also Kant's way of describing the kind of full commitment which characterizes religion, and such theology as Kant had, and which is contained in *Religion Within the Limits of Reason Alone*, is worked out in terms of this same key idea. In other words, that key idea which for Kant was anchored in moral commitment, is the same key idea by which Kant would interpret all theological phrases and doctrines—Christology, the Church, Sacraments, Prayer, and so on. Kant would not only parallel, he would identify religious commitment and dutiful behaviour.

Another parallel between dutiful behaviour and religious situations might be found by starting with Ross's notion of *prima facie* duties. There are on the one hand, Ross would say, the *prima facie* duties of promise-keeping, truth-telling, and the rest, duties which can be expressed in maxims and pre-

[1] Pp. 16-17.

cepts, and if a situation is characterized by more than one such *prima facie* duty, there is the familiar story of a conflict of duties. But in the end, out of such conflict, the *particular* duty (no longer *prima facie*) of a *particular* situation emerges, and it is this duty which in that *particular* situation would be given a parallel to that 'decisive' commitment which characterizes religious loyalty.

In all these ways then, by considering what moralists such as Butler, Kant and Ross have meant by 'acting from a sense of duty', we can find parallels to the commitment involved in religion, and the discernment in which it is founded. 'Conscience' (for Butler), the 'Moral Law' (for Kant) and 'Duty' (for Ross) are close logical kinsmen to the theologian's 'God', and give good approximations to its logical placing. It is not surprising that in the history of philosophy they have so often had the same enemies and the same friends.

Another illustration of religious 'commitment' can be seen in the loyalty which some have towards a school, a college, or a nation. It is well known that the philosopher McTaggart had, for instance, an intense loyalty for his College, and that this loyalty to the College, to its community, to his friends, inspired his metaphysics. For us that is significant. Here, for McTaggart, putting the point the other way round, was the kind of commitment which for him needed metaphysics, as for others it has needed theology to elucidate it.

Finally, let us round off our examples with a much lengthier one whose purpose is to hint even more pointedly, albeit still by parallels, at the character of that commitment which is distinctively religious.

We shall first comment on the kind of commitment involved in doing mathematics, something as distinct from religion as that. Thereafter we shall contrast with this kind of commitment the devotion we may give to a pastime, a ship or a person, and finally argue that religious commitment does something to unite the distinctive features of both kinds of loyalty.

Let us start then at a point which seems very distant from religion, viz. geometry. No doubt we all remember how we once proved that the three angles of a triangle were 180°. A triangle was drawn; its base produced at one corner, and at the same corner a line drawn parallel to the opposite side. Then, of the three angles making up the straight line at the corner—one is inside the triangle anyway, and the other two are respectively alternate and corresponding angles to the other two angles of the triangle. Thus the angles of the triangle, being equal to those of the straight line, are 180°.

Here is a typical example of mathematical reasoning, none the less typical for being specially simple. Each step follows indubitably from the one before—*but how do we start?* It might be said: with 'obvious axioms' that no one can doubt. But of course if we said that we would be wrong. The axioms of mathematics are only options and by now it is notorious that Euclid does not give us the only possible option—what of Lobatchewsky, Bolyai, Riemann, and the rest? In other words, when we claim to prove that the angles of a triangle are 180° what above all else we are doing is to display the starting point to which we have *committed* ourselves. Now two points about this mathematical 'commitment'.

(a) No mathematician *proves* his option. It is true that Form masters claim to 'prove' the axiom of parallels by taking little Jimmy to the front, asking him to walk along in a straight line; to turn through an angle and walk another way; then to turn through the same angle. Little Jimmy is then asked: 'And now you are walking in the same direction as before, aren't you?' to which is expected the answer, 'Yes.' But in doing all this, the Form master is not arguing; he is selling an option that in the form room is both plausible and reasonable. The fact that there is no argument about it becomes evident if little Jimmy hesitates, whereupon the master leaps in and says: 'Of course you are; you are bound to be.' But what would the master say to someone who asserted: 'I don't see it'? Only something abusive, I fear, like 'Oh, you wouldn't!'—and that very answer hints at the strange logical character of what is being commended, and shows how it is being commended in an appropriately odd way. Stories are being told, or scenes enacted in the hope that the light will dawn and the penny drop, that there will be 'insight', 'discernment', and the appropriate 'response' and 'commitment'.

(b) Secondly, let us notice that different starting points— different options—suit different circumstances. Build a house; construct a rectangular tennis court, and you will be wise to opt for Euclid. Work with inter-planetary space, or sub-atomic phenomena, and you will be wise to opt for something else.

What then does this mathematical example show? It shows that even in mathematical reasoning there is:

(i) A commitment involving options which are commended in odd ways.

(ii) This kind of commitment, with these different options, shows itself in correspondingly different axioms, different *posits* in relation to the language games—the different geometries—being played.

(iii) Here, nothing very serious is involved, nothing very violent occurs, when one posit is exchanged for another. There are no placard-bearers in mathematical departments with legends like 'There'll always be a Euclid', or 'Prepare to meet thy Riemann today'.

(iv) On the other hand, what is true, for example, of a Euclidian triangle, is true in Oxford and Cambridge, Moscow and New York, Mars and the moon. There is a broad catholicity about mathematics. No once correct assertion in pure mathematics is ever wrong, though it may not always be useful; and it may not always be adequate for understanding a particular situation. But once correct, it is correct everywhere, whether in Oxford, Cambridge, Moscow, New York, or elsewhere. What we are talking about when we talk of Euclidian triangles (and there would hang many difficulties) is, if we are once correct, correct everywhere. But the price to be paid for this universality is what we might call a very loose and problematical relation to 'facts'. Here of course (as I have said) arise many difficulties, but I do not want to complicate the example, and conclude it by emphasizing just one point: that mathematical posits express only a loose or partial commitment, though they have a universal use. Here then is a *partial* commitment extending to the *whole* universe.

Let us now look at something very different. Consider someone devoted (as we would say) to some pastime like cricket. A man's whole life may centre around it—it is the one subject of his conversation, his planning, his hopes. So much so that his language becomes coloured by it. Face him with some insoluble problem and he is 'stumped'; defeated on a committee he claims that his 'pitch has been queered'; violently disturbed over some moral or political situation, he claims that it's 'not cricket'. Here is his last stronghold; his basic protest; his court of final appeal. Here is a remark meant to cap every argument. Here indeed is a loyalty involving the whole of a man and expressible in terms of a key-word or cognate vocabulary.

Again, take a captain's devotion to his ship. So much so that in some disaster he sinks with it. Not because he is unwilling to face some sort of tribunal for mishandling it, as that he cannot bear to be parted from it. The ship is his life. All his thoughts, interests, hopes, centre around it; if it goes, he must go too. Once again, as in the cricket example, we have a total commitment to what . . . some *thing*? . . . no, the ship is personalized—'she'—so that it comes to be

34

paralleled with our total commitment to someone we love.

Which brings us very easily to our third example—
ἀγάπη, love, human affection; and I make no apologies
for putting them all together, since I am more interested in
the features they share than in the characteristics by which
they differ. Suppose someone says, 'I am longing to go to
Widnes,' and we say 'Why? It isn't that you like the dirt?'
'No.' 'The smell?' 'No.' 'The cold?' 'No.' 'The inaccessibility?'
'No.' We seek for an explanation but in vain. We say, 'You
must be mad.' But then the penny drops, the light dawns:
'*She's* there.' At once the whole circumstance is illuminated,
and we understand how our friend 'sees' Widnes: and so 'sees'
it that its dirt, smell, cold and inaccessibility, are organized
within a dominating loyalty. But the story can be taken
further. Suppose now 'she' has an accident, and is both
physically disfigured and psychologically maimed. Still, our
friend would go to Widnes, or I hope he would. If he didn't,
it wouldn't be ἀγάπη. What took him there would be
the same kind of feature about love which McTaggart
noticed when he remarked that a single smile or a look may
dominate our whole existence in its totality. Here is a commitment, a total commitment, with a strange empirical
relevance. Here is a commitment, a final option, which
organizes the whole of a man's life. Here, with similarities to,
but also differences from, the axioms of mathematics, is a
'posit' such as explanation games seek, something which
explanation harks after, something associated with what we
call 'insight', something whose anchorage is given when the
penny drops: 'she'.

So we come now to the main point. So far we have seen
two kinds of discernment-commitment—'mathematical'
commitment and 'personal' or 'quasi-personal' commitment. Religious commitment, I suggest, partakes of both. It
combines the total commitment to a pastime, to a ship, to a
person, with the breadth of mathematical commitment. It

combines the 'depth' of personal or quasi-personal loyalty—to a sport, a boat, a loved one—with the range of mathematical and scientific devotion. It is a commitment suited to the whole job of living—not one just suited to building houses, or studying inter-planetary motion, or even one suited to our own families, and no more.

Finally, we may remark that while religious commitment may thus be pictured as growing out of, and holding together 'mathematical' and 'personal' commitment, there are two ways in which it resembles the second kind of commitment we mentioned rather more than the first.

1. We say that cricket 'grips' us; the boat 'dominates' us; we 'fall' in love. Note the words: 'grips', 'dominates', 'fall'. We do not scheme ourselves, for instance, into love, or plan its every detail like a game that finishes at the chancel steps; or if we do, it is not love, however defensible or otherwise it may be as something else; for example, a scheme to obtain cheap domestic labour. Likewise, religious commitment is a response to something 'from outside us'—and the Christian for example can quote John 15.16: 'Ye have not chosen me, but I have chosen you. . . .'

2. Here is a commitment which we give up only at the cost of a personal revolution. We saw that we could embrace other mathematical options without any special heart-searching. But what of the cricket fan, the captain, the lover? He will always resist all attempts to break his loyalty. Take, for example, the lover. When people comment adversely on someone you love, it is a measure of your love as to how far you will resist the tales told to weaken your affection. But if in the end they succeed, the result is, not that we exchange without any heart-searching, one sort of 'axiom' for another—there is now a personal revolution, the whole of one's life is altered, we are 'converted', our 'vision' ceases. Here is something precisely parallel to religious commitment. If we have not been converted to it, we should certainly

36

have to be converted out of it; converted, as William James would have said, 'to infidelity'; when the world becomes 'flat'—lacking in 'depth'; vision and commitment disappear together.

So we see religious commitment as a *total* commitment to the *whole* universe; something in relation to which argument has only a very odd function; its purpose being to tell such a tale as evokes the 'insight', the 'discernment' from which the commitment follows as a response. Further, religious commitment is something bound up with key words whose logic no doubt resembles that of the words which characterize personal loyalty as well as that of the axioms of mathematics, and somehow combines features of both, being what might be called 'specially resistant' posits, 'final' endpoints of explanation, key-words suited to the whole job of living—'apex' words. In particular the Christian religion focuses such a cosmic commitment on Christ—on Christ as Jesus of Nazareth, born, dead and buried, but also on the risen and ascended Christ, the cosmic Christ of Ephesians and Colossians, the Christ who is organic to the old Israel and to the new Israel of his Church and through them to the whole of history.

But such reflections as these on this extended example have already brought us to the second major theme of this chapter: if our examples have done something to indicate the kind of empirical basis which belongs to religion, what do they tell us about religious language? If it be true that our examples have afforded some useful parallels for understanding what the religious man is talking about, the kind of distinctive situation to which the religious man appeals; if they have illustrated what we mean by talking of religion in terms of a discernment and a commitment: What do these examples suggest about religious language? What line do they give us on the structure of characteristically religious phrases? They suggest, I think, that religious language will

37

be logically odd in at least two ways, which are by no means unrelated, any more than are our two groups of examples.

I. If religious language has to talk about situations which bear great affinities to those we were discussing in the first group of examples, situations which are perceptual with a difference, perceptual and more, its language will be object language and more, i.e. object language which has been given very special qualifications, object language which exhibits logical peculiarities, logical impropriety. Now have we any general guide to this oddness, this impropriety? Well, does not the way in which distinctively *personal* situations parallel those which are *characteristically religious*, suggest close logical kinship between 'I' and 'God'? Both, by the standards of observational language, are odd in their logical behaviour. Take 'I'. Plainly 'I' is in part tractable in observational language—what 'I' refers to is not something entirely independent of our public behaviour. On the other hand, it can be argued, and all those who (like Hume himself) find Hume's 'object' theory of themselves inadequate will certainly argue that 'I' can never be exhausted by such language. So, if we wish to speak of everything which, for each of us, this 'I' refers to, we shall have to use phrases which—while beginning with and having some foothold in observational language—are somehow or other qualified to make it plain that their reference is in part beyond such language as well. The same is true about 'God'; and the central problem of theology is how to use, how to qualify, observational language so as to be suitable currency for what in part exceeds it—the situations in which theology is founded. At any rate, 'I' will never cease to be a useful guide for us when we are confronted with puzzles about 'God'.

If this is true in general, we would expect, for example, that some particular words in theological language would have the logic of nicknames—names where the 'object' reference is a minimum, and whose characteristic point is to evoke a distinctively personal relationship. The nickname, at once by its intelligibility and by its oddness, its suitability and impropriety, begins to be the closest public approximation of that 'I' for whose 'meaning' we would be seeking. The logic of nicknames may well give us some insight into some of the grammatical proper names used in theology. In any case we can expect the activity of naming in general to have a peculiar religious significance. For a person's 'name' claims to be, somehow, a public equivalent of what 'I' means to him.

Recalling next the tear in the dinner jacket—taking this as a non-verbal illustration—we might guess that theological language uses words which, like the dinner jacket, are for the most part recognizably straightforward, but in some way or other are (we might say) 'strained' to tell the tale.

The third example—swearing—suggests that theological language even when currency for a 'discernment', sometimes sponsors words which are key words for the whole of life. But as we have already anticipated in discussing commitment to axioms, to a pastime, to a ship or to a person, such key words are most characteristically carried by a *commitment*, and apart from noting that this reminds us that we cannot ultimately separate the twin features of the religious life, we will defer further comment on this example until we consider the suggestions about language which arise from the second group of examples.

Again, as the existentialist example was meant to make clear, the language appropriate to a characteristically theological situation may gain its oddness by typographical devices: when inverted commas, hyphens, or capital letters, are given to otherwise straightforward words. Or again, theological language may gain its oddness by using words 'technically' in the sense that a word is used very frequently in theological exposition without ever being itself elucidated, so that at best it gains a 'meaning in use'. As examples of the first kind of typographical qualification, we may take such phrases as 'authentic' and 'being-in-a-situation' as used by some existentialists; the second kind of oddness would be illustrated by words like 'existential' or for others, 'dialectical'.

Finally, the example of the Gestalt diagrams suggests that the oddness of theological language may arise, not so much from 'straining' ordinary language; not so much from qualifying it in some unusual way, but because of certain mixings of ordinary words, mixings of what at one time might have been called 'universes of discourse'. For the Gestalt diagram, by a certain mixing and juxtaposition of ordinary symbols—sides—manages to tell a tale which is more than a linear one, and to justify thereby an odd word like 'unity'.

II. Our second group of examples suggests that we may expect religious language to contain significant tautologies, tautologies whose function is to commend those key words— those ultimates of explanation—which, as we have already anticipated in our examples above, arise in connection with religious language, and especially with its character as a commitment.

To illustrate this contention, let us begin with the example of 'exercising free will'. Suppose someone asks us, with regard to a certain action X, where we would say we acted 'freely': 'Why did you do X?' It is true that we might as a first move give various reasons of a straightforward kind, specifying one causal antecedent or another. But coming nearer and nearer to the event, the ultimate reason would always be: 'Because I chose to do X.' If we were further questioned: 'Why did you choose to do X?' the only possible move, apart from yet another retrospective sequence of causal antecedents—and now the psychoanalyst might come in with his story—would be to say 'Because I chose to do it'—'Because I'm I'— tautologies. Let me give a specific example to develop this point in more detail. There are two different ways in which a man Smith may rise at 4 a.m. First, when called, he may open his eyes but remain stationary. On this alternative he only gets up when he is forcibly ejected from his bed. No one would wish to say that in any sense this was a 'free' action. His getting up is the result of certain forces brought to bear upon him, and if we ask him later in the day, 'Why did you get up at four this morning?' the answer would always begin —'Because Jones threw me out of bed at that hour'; and however many more questions were asked, their answers would always permit of other questions of the same form.

But suppose in the second case that the man is called at four and responds 'freely'. Later in the day we ask 'Why did you get up at four?' The answer might be: 'Because I wished to have breakfast early.' We then continue: 'Why did you wish to have breakfast early?' Answer: 'Because I wished to get a bus.' 'Why did you wish to get a bus?' 'Because I wished to go fishing.' 'Why did you wish to go fishing?' 'Because I wanted to fish.' 'Why did you want to fish?' 'What a question! You know what fishing is for me. Fishing is fishing.' 'Why did I want to fish? Because I'm I.' An answer of the same 'final' form might have been given at the start. To our question: 'Why did you get up at four?' the reply could have been made: 'Because I chose to do, and that's the person I happen to be.' Here is a position quite different from any we would reach in the other case when the man is thrown out of bed. In the case of a 'free' response we reach a position in the question-answer game beyond which no move is possible along the same lines. There has been declared for that particular question-answer game, a 'final option'. Fishing is something not to be questioned; it is something which exerts an authoritative claim on the person in question. It was in response to this claim—the 'discernment', the 'obligation' that fishing brings with it—that Smith acted 'freely' when he rose at four. When Smith says that 'Fishing is fishing', he is expressing the fact that 'fishing' represents for him an obligation, a focus of loyalty, an object of 'discernment', to which he has made a 'free' response. To the tautology which expresses the claim of the 'object': 'Fishing is fishing', there can be paralleled that tautology which expresses the subjective response: 'I'm I.' This fact could be seen if somebody said: 'I cannot understand why anyone should have such a devotion to fishing; I cannot understand why anyone would rise so early to fish; I see nothing in fishing myself,' and so on. Smith would reply that 'one man's meat is another man's poison', and that fishing was, for him, that on which his whole life was centred. 'Fishing' and 'I' would be for him kinsmen. Whereupon 'Fishing is fishing' becomes an objective counterpart of 'I'm I'.

As we would expect from our other examples, the language of morals reveals similar tautologies which are means of commending key words and final options. We recall immediately the precept: 'Duty for duty's sake'. Here is a tautology which is commending 'duty' as a key word for existence. Consequently we can see the odd character of the question: 'Why do your duty?' at any rate for those who would sponsor a morality of 'Duty for duty's sake'. For them this question would be in any straightforward sense unanswerable. To 'Why do your duty?', the answer would be 'Because it is my duty', or 'Duty is duty', and once again we would have a tautology disclosing a final option, an 'irreducible posit'. Here would be a key word embodied in a tautology, and expressive of a total commitment. To the question 'Why do your duty?' the only satisfactory answer would thus be to evoke in the questioner the 'sense of duty' which the tautology is meant to express and evoke. 'Why do your duty?' is only 'answered' by showing what 'duty' specifies. It then answers itself.

The same point could be made by considering how Butler used the word 'conscience'. Had it power as it has authority, it would rule the world. Its realm is all-embracing. Its authority is 'ultimate'—all extensive. If anyone asks: 'Why obey conscience?', the answer can only be: 'Because conscience is conscience.' Once again we have a tautology sponsoring a key word and declaring a commitment; and our questioner is only satisfactorily answered when we display this commitment on some occasion 'of great consequence'. He then 'sees' what conscientious behaviour is; and recognizes his question for the pseudo-question it was.

Further, it is important, from the point of view of religious language which must do justice to 'discernment' as well as to 'commitment', to notice that the key words which are commended in tautologies which are currency for commitment, do not themselves belong to ordinary perceptual language. So justice is done to both features of religion at once. For instance, those who have wished to commend 'duty' as a key-word, those who have sponsored the tautology 'Duty for duty's sake', have often then said that when a man does his duty, he acts 'independently of consequences'. This, I suggest, has been a very misleading way of claiming that a 'dutiful' situation has a certain spatio-temporal elusiveness; that a morally obligable situation will never be exhausted by those perceptual terms which are its 'consequences'. What should be said is that no number of spatio-temporal events can ever exhaust what we mean by 'duty', though in asserting this we must not suggest (as some intuitionists may have done) that duty is altogether independent of the spatio-temporal behaviour it elicits. My point is, that to say 'Duty is independent of consequences', is to claim, however misleadingly, that 'duty' relates to a situation which cannot be altogether unpacked in the language of perceptual resultants, but is recognized with the kind of discernment like that which we have called 'characteristically religious'.

The same point could be made by recalling Kant's nervousness at allowing any kind of connection between the moral law and pleasure. He was so impressed by the difference between a 'moral', 'dutiful', 'virtuous' situation on the one hand, and a 'pleasure' situation on the other; he saw so plainly the distinctive difference which there is between 'following the moral law' and 'following pleasure', that in effect he claimed that between the 'moral law' and 'pleasure' no straightforward logical link could be forged. It was indeed, as is well known, only forged for Kant in terms of the problematical word 'God'—this is his 'moral argument'; it was only forged when, in this way, commitment to God was shown as something which could include within itself both the commitment expressed in following the moral law, and the pleasure which on occasion, but otherwise only *de facto* accompanied dutiful action. But devotion to God, for Kant, involves no more 'discernment' than is involved in our 'respect' for the moral law. Devotion to God may be broader than devotion to duty, but for Kant, as we saw, religion involves no greater 'insight' than a 'sense of duty' already gives us.

In all these ways, then, examples from morality suggest that if they command key-words the tautologies of religion will be apt currency for its *commitment*; and that such key-words, when they are from the standpoint of perceptual language, 'odd', will also be apt currency for *discernment* as well. Certainly, it has often happened that 'Duty' and 'Conscience' have been given logical placings very similar to that of 'God'. When people speak of 'duty' in terms of 'God's will', or of 'conscience' as 'God's voice', I suggest that they are making precisely this claim for logical kinship, and what we have said may perhaps illuminate the logical structure of the complex claim they are making.

On this point of logical kinsmen for 'God', let us recall how in the loyalty to a ship or a person, to a college, school or nation, we found a parallel to religious commitment. It is then not surprising that this loyalty is sometimes expressed

in phrases which like those of theology have their own peculiar logic, e.g. 'My country right or wrong'. If this is taken
to be no more than an ethical assertion, it is plainly open to
the gravest difficulties. But if it is a way of insisting that the
loyalty to a nation may be something even greater than one
which is expressed in moral words, then—though the claim
may be open to argument—it is not obviously silly, and certainly not self-contradictory. The same sort of claim is in
fact now being made about a 'nation' that intuitionists have
made for 'duty' when they have declared it 'independent of
consequences', or Kant made for the 'moral law' when he
distinguished it from 'pleasure'. In other words, 'My country
right or wrong', is a way of representing and proclaiming a
dominant loyalty to a nation, in which case 'country' for the
'absolute' patriot would have a logical placing very similar
to 'God' for the theist.

After all this, I need do no more than recall briefly that
parallel to theological 'key-words' are also the axioms of
mathematics, reached when questions have pushed us to the
'irreducible posits' of a particular system. These express in
tautologies, in necessary propositions, the loyalty, the option
of the mathematician, as he posits the particular conventions.
There is perhaps a closer relation between 'doing mathematics' and 'being religious' than we had supposed. Descartes
and Spinoza may not have been wrong in their hunch that
mathematics and metaphysics were closely related: their
mistake was to suppose them identical.

So to some concluding remarks. We should expect religious
language, we have said, to be constructed from object
language which has been given appropriately strange qualifications, and in other chapters we shall examine particular
ways in which such qualifications may be made. But already
we might make a few general reflections. For example, it is
sometimes asked: how can religious people speak of a 'sense'
of what is 'unseen'? But if the moralists speak of a 'sense' of

'duty', why should not the religious person speak of a 'sense' of the 'unseen'? In each of these phrases a word with a perfectly good meaning in perceptual language—'sense'—is given a qualification of such a kind that the ensuing phrase seems to be bogus, if not self-contradictory. So can parallels to the impropriety of religious language be found in other areas, and if apparent nonsense is repeated in places widely apart, we shall be hesitant before we say that such phrases are entirely devoid of meaning.

We may also expect religious language to centre on 'God' as a key word, an 'ultimate' of explanation, which becomes the subject of significant tautologies. Once again we shall be giving examples in other chapters, but one might just be worth a mention here. We all know how the phrase 'God is Love' has been criticized as being a platitude, because it is alleged to say nothing. But may not this be because it has the logical form of a tautology? If so, we misunderstand it if we do not see it as a *significant* tautology labelling a commitment. In this way the logical structure of the phrase 'God is Love' would be something as follows: We should have to tell a story of human devotion until a characteristically religious situation was evoked. We should have to tell the stories of the 'lives of good men' until a point was reached where we did not merely admire the 'goodness' or try to express it in some precept, but where, when the characteristic 'discernment' was evoked, we responded with a total commitment: 'Love so amazing, so divine, demands my soul, my life, my all.' It would be in relation to such a situation that the religious man would then posit the word 'God' or the word 'Love'. To say that 'God is Love' is thus to claim that the word 'God' can be given in relation to a total commitment (*alternatively labelled 'Love'*) which can be approached by considering those partial commitments which we normally describe in terms of the word 'love'. All this raises, of course, but leaves untouched, the question as to the relation between

46

the 'Love' which is a synonym for 'God', and the 'love' of ordinary language.

Certainly we must carefully distinguish 'God is Love' from 'God is loving'. This latter assertion cannot be left without some kind of qualification, for, as it stands, it predicates of God a word—'loving'—which belongs to ordinary straightforward language. Not surprisingly, then, the more typical and satisfactory theological assertion would be: 'God is infinitely loving', a phrase with a particular logical structure which we shall be considering presently. All we need say for the moment is that here is a qualification of the kind we noticed in relation to our first group of examples, and that the 'Love', which as a logical synonym for 'God' gives the tautology 'God is Love', is equivalent to 'infinite love', which (as we shall see) is as logically distant from 'love' as 'infinite sum' for the mathematician is distant from 'sum'. 'God is Love', then, is a significant tautology pleading 'Love' (or 'God') as a commitment word.

So our conclusion is that for the religious man 'God' is a key word, an irreducible posit, an ultimate of explanation expressive of the kind of *commitment* he professes. It is to be talked about in terms of the object-language over which it presides, but only when this object-language is qualified; in which case this qualified object-language becomes also currency for that odd *discernment* with which religious *commitment*, when it is not bigotry or fanaticism, will necessarily be associated.

Meanwhile, as a corollary, we can note that to understand religious language or theology we must first evoke the odd kind of situation to which I have given various parallels above. This is plainly a *sine qua non* for any religious apologetic.

At the same time we must train ourselves to have a nose for odd language, for 'logical impropriety', and it is possible to do this by concerning ourselves with other examples of odd language which may not in the first instance be religious. Of such language, poetry is plainly an example. On the other hand, the person who by inclination is more scientific than poetical, might well look for the odd words and phrases which his scientific theories, if broad enough in their reference, will throw up. Such words range from 'absolute space' for Newton, to 'continuous creation' for Hoyle, not forgetting the all-embracing use of 'evolution' in the later nineteenth century. Words such as these will certainly have an 'odd' logical behaviour compared with those which are contained in the more straightforward generalizations which the theory incorporates, and which can, in a fairly obvious sense, be 'verified'. I am not saying for a moment that the language of poetry, or the odd phrases of science, have in every respect the logical behaviour which would justify them in being called religious. But I am saying that a useful antidote to the craze for straightforward language might be found in suitable doses of poetry or greater familiarity with the curiously odd words thrown up in scientific theories. Such doses would at any rate begin to suggest to us that there is an important place for odd language; that odd language may well have a distinctive significance, and we might even conclude in the end that the odder the language the more it matters to us.

II

SOME TRADITIONAL CHARACTERIZATIONS OF GOD: MODELS AND QUALIFIERS

IN the previous chapter I said that our intention was to see something of the implications for theology, of the concern of contemporary philosophy with language and empirical fact. Taking Butler as a classical example, I tried to show that religious language talks of the discernment with which is associated, by way of response, a total commitment. We then noticed that parallels to this *discernment*, which yields more than 'what's seen', could be found in situations which 'come alive', where 'the penny drops', or 'the ice breaks', where we discover a person's name, and so on. I suggested that parallels to the *commitment* which characterizes religion, might be found in the devoted action of a 'free will'; in action from a 'sense of duty', and also in the loyalty we give to persons, institutions and nations. Altogether the total commitment of religion might be said roughly to take such deep personal loyalty as we have exemplified and to give it the breadth of such commitment as that by which the mathematician embraces his axioms.

Our broad conclusion was that if this discernment-commitment is the kind of situation characteristic of religion, we must expect religious language to be appropriately odd, and to have a distinctive logical behaviour. Otherwise it would not be currency for the strange kind of situation about which it claims to speak. In this second chapter we shall discuss some special examples of this distinctive logical

49

behaviour of religious language—in particular some phrases about God and his attributes. How do we talk about God? How do those words work that profess to talk about God and his attributes? What logical moves does such talking involve? I propose to take three groups of examples to see some of the answers which might be given to questions such as these. We shall consider in order:

(i) The attributes of negative theology: such as 'immutable', 'impassible'.

(ii) The characterization of God by 'Unity', 'Simplicity', 'Perfection'.

(iii) Other traditional attributes and characterizations: e.g., *'First* CAUSE', *'Infinitely* WISE'; *'Infinitely* GOOD'; 'CREATOR *ex nihilo'*; *'eternal* PURPOSE'.

(i) *First then, the attributes of negative theology.*

My suggestion is that we understand their logical behaviour aright if we see them as primarily evocative of what we have called the odd discernment, that characteristically religious situation which, if evoked, provokes a total commitment. Let us now develop that suggestion, and first recall that this discernment yields more than 'what's seen'. It occurs when we are aware of something more than the spatio-temporal features of a particular situation; when a particular situation is perceptual *and more.*

Now two characteristic features of all perceptual situations are (a) change, and (b) the inter-action which change seems to presuppose. The attributes of negative theology fix on such characteristics of perceptual situations, and whisper in our ears a contrasting denial: Change? Yes, but there's something which does not change, which is 'immutable'. . . . Change? But *not everything* changes: *not everything* is obliterated as a situation is transformed: Or, confronted with interaction, the whisper now is 'impassible' . . . interaction is not the whole story. Let me illustrate with two examples:

50

(1) Let us imagine that we are travelling by train in a remote district as darkness falls. Little by little the scene is obliterated; first trees, then houses, slowly disappear from view; then the pylons, then the particular folds of the hills; then the hills themselves. Darkness has fallen: 'Fast falls the eventide'; 'the darkness deepens'. Change (if not decay) in all around I see. Now at every point in this changing scene, 'immutability', as an attribute of negative theology, whispers to us: 'But not everything changes. . . . Is there not something which is unchanged? Do you not apprehend something which remains invariable in the situation despite what is so visibly changing?' . . . Such suggestions are constantly repeated as the scene constantly changes, in the hope that at some point or other the penny will drop, the ice break, the light dawn; that there will break on us that 'discernment' which is a 'sense of the unseen', a characteristically-religious situation, to which 'immutability' has led us.

Or again, we meet an old friend whom we have not seen for many years. The freshness of youth has been replaced by the lines of age; black hair by grey, and so on. We are inclined to say 'How much you have changed'. But such an attribute of negative theology as 'immutable' would then whisper to us: 'Yet something is the same.' Has not 'the bond of friendship' remained firm, invariable, fixed, despite the changes and chances and all that has been transitory? In discerning this 'bond' which, despite all change, had remained constant, we should have found another example of what we have called an 'odd discernment'. So does 'immutability' lead us to God, for it is in situations such as this that people have spoken of 'seeing God' in their love for a friend.

(2) Let us now take a parallel example which considers not change as such, but the *interaction* which change presupposes, and by fixing on this feature of any perceptual situation, let us see how the situation can be so developed

that once again an odd discernment is evoked. Fix, then, on 'passibility' and develop it in a story: it might be alleged, for example, that we are all products of our environment, that we suffer from economic forces which determine all our work, intentions, hopes, lives and so on. Others may say that we are nothing but a battle-ground of instincts and psychological 'forces' of one sort and another. Now in so far as such assertions are made on the basis of careful experiment or investigation, plainly they cannot be gainsaid. In so far as they show the extent to which our lives are determined by economic forces; the extent to which they can be treated in terms of the concepts of psychology and so on, who would wish necessarily to deny them? Only if it were claimed for any such account that it completely exhausted us and our behaviour, would battle be joined. This leads us to see just how the word 'impassible' behaves. What the word 'impassible' does is to whisper in our ear: Passible? Yes, of course . . . of course. . . . Certainly there is interaction written over the universe; certainly there is 'suffering' whether in that technical sense, or in one which is more distinctively and sadly human . . . *but* this is not the whole story; 'passible' is not the last word, interaction does not say everything, suffering leaves more to be said. So 'impassible' invites us to treat all 'passible' stories as inadequate; to agree with all the positive points they make and to invite them to go yet further—for what purpose? Until at some point or other once again the light dawns, the ice breaks, the penny drops; until an 'odd discernment' is evoked. As with F. H. Bradley when time and time again 'terms and relations' stories, in this case interaction stories, have 'failed to satisfy' there may then be evoked at some point what he called 'immediate experience', a logical synonym for what we call an 'odd discernment'. It is then that we speak of even suffering as 'fulfilled' and 'transformed' to give 'insight' and 'peace'.

So when we talk of God as 'immutable', or as 'impassible',

52

the function of these particular attribute-words is primarily to evoke the kind of situation we have just been mentioning; to fix on mutable and passible features of perceptual situations and to develop these features in such a way that there is evoked a characteristically different situation which is the foundation *in fact* for assertions about God's immutability or impassibility. But there is a little more to it than that. For these words 'immutability' and 'impassibility' make also a *language* plea. They claim for the word 'God' a position outside all mutable and passible language. Beyond that negative claim the attributes of negative theology do not however go. All they tell us is that if anything is 'mutable' it will not be exact currency for God; that if anything is 'passible' it will not be exact currency for God. So the main merit of attribute words like 'immutable' and 'impassible' is to give a kind of technique for meditation; their main merit is evocative. Anticipating a distinction we shall develop in our third group of examples, we might say that here we have one of the simplest examples of a 'model' and a 'qualifier', where, in this instance, the qualifier is hardly more than an operator, (i.e. *im-*) which develops and evokes the characteristic situation from the basis of a particular model, e.g. mutability or passibility. Features of perceptual situations are progressively obliterated in an endeavour to bring about that discernment which is the basis for talking about God. But the very fact that the characteristic situation is reached in this way, means that we have specified God only at the cost of emphasizing his distance from certain characterizations of perceptual language. We are told next to nothing as to how we can use the word 'God' significantly.

(ii) Now we come to our second group of examples where we consider the characterization of God in terms of 'Unity', 'Simplicity', 'Perfection'. What account of the logical behaviour of these words can we give?

I suggest that such words as these make use of what we

might call the method of contrasts. According to this method, if we are puzzled as to what a word means, when it has nevertheless some various associations for us, it is sometimes a help to see if we can name an opposite and so, indirectly, try to get the meaning of the first word by having before us a situation which contrasts with that which we wish to understand.

Take for example the case of unity. We are puzzled as to what exactly the word means, so we try its opposite, viz. diversity—'the many'. According to this technique we approach the meaning of 'unity' by seeing what happens to a diverse situation when we try to get rid of the diversity, when the diversity is progressively removed, when the many are progressively unified. There is, for instance, in our room —a table, a chair, a carpet, and so on. Such diversity we endeavour to overcome by what Bradley would call 'relational addition from without'. In other words, we try to overcome this diversity by seeing them all as related to each other and to other objects such as pictures, all within one room. But then there are *many* rooms; so once again we endeavour to overcome the diversity by 'one house'. But then there are *many* houses, and to remove the diversity now we must think of a city. From a city comes a multiplicity of cities, and the counter-move is to think of a county; from a county we think of a country, and so on and so on. The story must be told and continue to be told until there breaks in on us at some point a situation characteristically different from its predecessors; until at some point or other the penny drops, the light dawns, there is a characteristic 'disclosure' and there is evoked that situation in relation to which the word 'unity' is to be commended.

If the reader complains that the penny is unlikely to drop unless he is Bradley-minded, with some sort of idealist weakness for metaphysics, we may usefully recall that even an empiricist like Russell on occasion wishes to talk about 'unities': and that when he does he has in mind the same kind of situation we have been trying to evoke. For instance, Russell is concerned to show[1] that something we might call a 'unity' is involved when a child learns the use of a word as distinct from knowing the letters within it. In other words, a child may know the letter 'C'; he may know the letter 'A'; he may know the letter 'T'; but when he places these three together C-A-T and says at the end, 'cat', there is (or so *we* would say) a situation characteristically different from those which preceded it, and a situation very similar to that to which we appeal when we use the word 'unity' of God. It may be of course that when the child arrives at the letter 'T', a characteristic situation does not break in on him, the penny does not drop, the bell does not ring, and so on, in which case, if we wanted to teach someone what was involved in the meaning of 'unity' we should have to continue the enumeration, just as in the case of other stories about diversity. We should, for example, have to try such words as C-a-t-a-l-y-s-t, or C-a-t-a-c-o-m-b, and if these failed, we might try C-a-t-a-s-t-r-o-p-h-e.

At any rate, if anyone wishes to know what is meant by predicating 'unity' of God, the first thing we have to do is to evoke such a characteristic situation as we have indicated, and I have suggested that we can do this in particular, by the method of contrasts, which endeavours progressively to negative stories of diversity.

The same technique applies to 'simplicity'. Once again, we take its opposite—'complexity'. But this time I suggest that we try to get rid of complexity, not by addition from without, but by analysis from within. For instance, we might start with some complex fact such as a car. To deny its complexity we analyse: we endeavour to break it up, to take it to pieces, and by such a process we finish with

[1] Bertrand Russell: *An Inquiry into Meaning and Truth*, pp. 335-6, Allen & Unwin, 1940.

relatively simple parts. But any of these 'simple' parts, for example the carburetter, can immediately be broken down into simpler parts, and still the search for simplicity can go on. Now the reader might say: What happens when we come to nothing but an iron rod half an inch long? Surely this is 'simple'? In one obvious sense it is, but not in the sense we are after when we want to speak of the 'simplicity' of God. To arrive at that sense the story must go on and now we should have to make some sort of move to the language of chemistry. This apparently 'simple' rod, we should now talk of in terms of molecules, after molecules would come atoms, and after atoms electrons, and the important point is *never* to halt the story if we can still go further, and the characteristic situation has not yet broken. For without such a situation we cannot rightly speak of God in terms of 'simplicity'.

In parenthesis, it is important to notice that when the situation does break in on us, we do not properly label it with the word we have just uttered to describe the latest member of the sequence of 'simple' parts. For example, we may have arrived at the word 'atom', and at this point the disclosure may have been made, and we may be then tempted to think that the word 'atom' appropriately belongs to and names this characteristically different situation. But not so. The word 'atom' is part of the straightforward story which has led to the significantly different situation, and we shall want language of a significantly different kind to do justice to it. If we use the word 'atom' as appropriate currency for the disclosure, it will only be by using 'atom' differently from the way in which it was used in the story—an ambiguity that is bound in the end to lead to the confusion it has done. Some people, for example, being gifted with scientific insight, and having had a 'disclosure' at some point or other in relation to a scientific story, have then taken the last word in the scientific story as being appropriate to the full insight which had been evoked. But if the word 'atom' is in this way altogether appropriate, it does not belong to the scientific story. Rather could we say (for example) that 'atom' in this case behaves like 'God' for the theist. It may be, as Carruthers' poem has it, that when a disclosure occurs 'some call it Evolution, and others call it God'; but if so, and if my contention is right, 'evolution' is *not* then a word working entirely according to the rules of scientific language. Its behaviour must be different enough to do justice to the idiosyncracy of the new situation.

Lastly, let us consider the characterization of God by 'perfection'. Once again, if we use the method of contrasts we begin with 'imperfections' which we try to remove. Imagine that we are walking by a hedge on a September afternoon and see blackberries small and dusty just below shoulder height and easy to grasp. Then, right at the top of the hedge and almost out of reach, we see some which are much less imperfect. Eventually after long struggles we pick these better blackberries, but the wet blanket of the party tells us that they are as nothing compared with those he found in a lane in Somerset five years ago; whereupon an even greater blackberry genius comes along and says that those in Somerset were as nothing compared with those collected in Wiltshire in 1897; but, says the B.B.C. expert, were not all these imperfect compared with the prize-winning exhibit at Nether Wallop Summer Fête in 1851 ? So we have been led from the obvious imperfection, to less imperfection, and thereafter to still less imperfection, until at some point or other (I hope) a disclosure occurs, a characteristic situation dawns in relation to which we would use words like 'ideal' or 'perfection'. But there would be no 'ideal' or 'perfect' blackberry. 'Ideal' or 'perfect' become now logical kinsmen not of 'blackberries' but of 'God', a word appropriate to what is given to us in a situation which no stories of seeing, touching, smelling, tasting, can ever exhaust.

It might be said that in contrast to unity and simplicity,

the idea of perfection is much more easily grasped so that the method of contrasts (which we have just used) is neither so needful nor useful. Certainly it can here be easily avoided, as we shall now show. 'Perfection?' we say—'oh yes; that's not too difficult to understand.' There comes immediately to mind 'the best man I ever knew', X, whom we call a 'saint'. But then someone comes along and says: 'I am sure X is a saint', but he'd be all the better for being a good 'administrator'. So we then think of the good administrators we know, and in particular we recall Y, an excellent headmaster, a most competent administrator, who is all these and also a saint. Is this perfection? Not at all, we are told. Bishop Z has all the excellence of Y, but a perfect man would be a better bishop. Then we think of B, who is not only a saint, a good administrator, has all the qualities of the 'perfect' Bishop—friendly, cheerful, and human, with a strong sense of pastoral duty and so on. But people will say, B may be all that, but he is not 'devout'. It will then be retorted: how can he fail to be 'devout' if he is a 'saint'? And the conversation will now begin to fix on senses of sanctity which might not imply 'being devout', and so on. How long should such stories go on, and what could be their point? The story will have to go on until, at one and the same time, there dawns on us the futility of ever hoping to get a cut-and-dried description of 'perfection', and a situation was evoked which somehow or other presented to us the 'perfection', the 'ideal', after which we were searching. Once again a story would have been developed until a characteristic disclosure was evoked.

It is obvious that all these examples follow very much the pattern of those by which we elucidated the attributes of negative theology. But in this second group of examples when the word 'God' is posited, a much more express claim about theological language becomes possible. We may not yet be able to say all we want to say about God; but we can say much more about him than we could by means of the attributes of negative theology. For not only do these words 'unity', 'simplicity', 'perfection', work as we have indicated to evoke the appropriate *fact*; or, better, the appropriate *situation*; they each make an important claim about theological language; they have each a claim to make about the word 'God'. To talk of God in terms of 'unity' means, if we translate this into the formal mode, that the word 'God' *unites* all the diversity of language which is used to talk about the world around us. 'Simplicity' claims that the word 'God' effects this unity as a *single* word which presides as a sort of key word over the whole of language. To speak of God in terms of 'perfection' does something to develop what has been already said, for the suggestion now is that the word 'God', by uniting the diverse strands of language in a single word, 'completes' any one of these language strands which talks about its subject the more precisely only according as that subject is the more 'imperfect', or (shall we say?) 'abstract'. In other words, the claim made for 'God' by these characterizations of 'Unity', 'Simplicity', 'Perfection', is that 'God' is a key word presiding over the whole of language and suited to a total commitment. What this claim in detail involves, and how the word 'presides' over the rest of language, is a complex logical story which cannot be developed here beyond giving two examples, which may perhaps illuminate it somewhat.

Suppose we have a mathematical sequence of sums: $S_0 = 1$; $S_1 = 1 + \dfrac{1}{2}$; $S_2 = 1 + \dfrac{1}{2} + \dfrac{1}{2^2}$; $S_3 = 1 + \dfrac{1}{2} + \dfrac{1}{2^2} + \dfrac{1}{2^3}$, etc. We see at once that S_2 may be said to be 'imperfect' compared with S_3, and in the same way any S—say S_r—might be said to be 'imperfect' compared with $S_r + 1$. As the sums develop we may in fact say that they become less and less 'imperfect'.

Now in so far as these sums move progressively towards 2

without ever reaching it, 2 may be said to 'complete' all these sums and to preside over the various imperfect sums which somehow or other it holds together. In this way a limit word in mathematics may offer some parallel to the word 'God' in theology, when we speak of that word presiding over and unifying the languages of empirical imperfection. What then corresponds to the complex logical story in theology (which we have excused ourselves from attempting here) would be the logical theory of limits in mathematics, which explains, and in detail, just how the word 2 comes to be associated with such a succession of sequences as we have mentioned.

Our second example comes from philosophy. To say that the word 'God' presides over the rest of language is to claim that logically it has the same kind of status as Hegel gave to the word 'Absolute' or 'Absolute Spirit'. On this parallel, just as for Hegel (if he were right) we would always, as a matter of logical necessity, and by a firm logical route, reach the word 'Absolute' no matter where we began, so the theist would claim that the word 'God' would always be reached from any starting point if we persevered with the logical route long enough. In this series it 'completes' and 'presides over' the rest of language. We may not at all wish to think of categories spread out in a dialectical pattern as Hegel believed, but I suggest that broadly his point was sound, and that (for the theist) the word 'God' may be pictured as the centre of a maze—the spot where we finally arrive if we walk long enough and make the correct logical moves.

So once again theological words specifying the attributes of God are understood when a characteristic situation is evoked and an appropriate language claim is made; though we have seen that in talking about God, words like 'unity', 'simplicity', 'perfection', take us somewhat further than did the attributes of negative theology. But the most useful phrases of all are in the next and last group. Whereas all the words we have discussed so far could evoke reasonably well the kind of situation to which we must refer when we wish to speak of God: the merit of this last group is that it gives us the fullest insight as to how theology is built out of ordinary language; it helps us most of all if we ask: just how oddly do theological phrases use ordinary words?

(iii) In this last group I propose to discuss five examples: First Cause, Infinitely Wise, Infinitely Good, Creation *ex nihilo*, and Eternal Purpose. In every case I hope to show just what logical structure these phrases have when they appeal to the kind of situation we have called characteristically religious.

1. *'First* CAUSE*'*

What is such a phrase claiming when it is predicated of God? In what kind of situation can it be given an empirical anchorage? My suggestion is this.

(a) Of these two words, one, the word 'cause', gives us a 'model'. Now, what is a 'model' in this context? It is a situation with which we are all familiar, and which can be used for reaching another situation with which we are not so familiar; one which, without the model, we should not recognize so easily. The word 'cause', I say, specifies a particular situation. It starts us with this tree, or this piece of coal, or this human being, and puts them in a causal setting. We can think, for example, of this tree in relation to the acorn from which it came; or this tree as over a long period of time and under certain pressures becoming coal. Again, we can think of this coal when it was a tree, and (if we are lucky) when it is burning and giving out heat. We can trace the causal development either way. With a human being we think at once of causal ancestors and causal successors. Here then we are given, by means of the word 'cause', specific straightforward pictures.

(b) Now in relation to such models the word 'first' has a

special function in virtue of which it might be called a 'Qualifier'. It is a directive which prescribes a special way of developing those 'model' situations. It suggests that when presented with a tree we do not think of coal, but rather of a seed; when we think of coal we do not think of fires but of prehistoric forests; when we think of human beings we do not think of future generations but of ancestors and environment. In short, the word 'first' presses us to move backward and still backward, and because the causal story is such as can keep us going as long as anyone wishes, the directive 'backward and still backward' is always able to be obeyed. As with our earlier examples, we are directed to continue the story to build up a pattern of terms and relations until a characteristically different situation is evoked: a situation which in Bradley's phrase 'satisfies'; when the light dawns, the penny drops, the ice breaks. At that point there is a 'sense of the unseen', what is sometimes called 'a sense of mystery'. Here is something 'mysterious' which eludes the grasp of causal language. This is not 'mystery' that a further development of the causal story could eradicate; not 'mystery' which a continuation of the story will overcome as it had done before; not 'mystery' if this is taken to be a synonym for ignorance. For the causal story could always go on further to eradicate 'mystery' in this sense. It could always be developed to meet any further query: any request for further information. But if we are to do justice to theology there must be 'mystery' in another sense whereby a situation is 'mysterious' when it is what's seen, what's talked about in causal language, *and more*. So the causal game is played until at some point or other a characteristically different situation is evoked. When that happens, it is in relation to such a situation that the word 'God' would be posited. With what kind of logical placing? This brings us to our next point.

For when the situation breaks in on us, the word 'first' has another function. When 'first cause' leads us to posit 'God' according to the procedure we have so far been describing, it claims at the same time that the word 'God' 'completes' causal stories; is 'logically prior' to such stories, is the 'first' word of them. Now what do we mean by a word being 'first' in this sense? What is here being claimed for its logical status?

To give some kind of answer to this question, though in the nature of the case it cannot be a full one, let us imagine a swimming pool. Someone is diving. We might ask about a certain point between the spring-board and the pool: why is this toe at this point moving thus? Such a question might lead to a succession of causal answers. This toe is moving in this direction with this velocity because a moment ago it was moving in that direction with that velocity; and it was moving in that direction with that velocity because a moment before that it was moving in such and such a direction with such and such velocity. So the causal story would continue, taking us back until the spring-board was reached, and there, when we asked: 'Why did this toe move in that direction with that velocity?' the swimmer's answer could be: 'Because I decided to dive.' If now we asked: 'Why did you decide to dive?' it would always be possible to answer: 'Because I wanted to'; and if we questioned that—saying, for instance, that the morning was so cold and frosty; that no one has been known to use the pool at this time of the year, and so on; how could anyone *want* to dive in all those circumstances? the only kind of answer to our scepticism (and we recall a similar case in Chapter I) would be 'I'm I'. Here would be something emphatic and final. Here is what we might call a logical stop-card. Somehow, at the spring-board, a different logical move can be made, and it is when this kind of move is made that we talk of the causal story being 'completed'.

Of course, from another point of view, the causal story might never be completed. At the spring-board various other causal moves become admittedly possible. We ask: 'Why did you decide to dive?' Now if we had been reading all about the Oedipus complex we might then tell some startling causal story which related to the man's father who was a prize-winning diver at some seaside resort. Or we might say that the man decided to dive because of a desire to 'display', knowing that his girl friend was on the other side of the pool. Others more anthropologically minded might talk of the 'uprush of a primitive jumping instinct' and so on. But all these would be causal stories proceeding along independent routes of their own, each making the same kind of inroad into that spring-board situation which was reached for us along the particular route of causal sequence with which we began. In other words, no matter how many of these causal stories could be adduced as 'answers' to the question: 'Why did that toe move with that velocity in that direction from the spring-board?', none of them follows of unique *necessity* from, or is continuously linked with, the particular causal story we were tracing earlier. None of them does anything to challenge the logical difference of the answer 'Because I decided to dive', which is logically different from them all. Indeed, they are all alternative routes converging on the same point, and in this sense they could all be regarded as unpacking in their own way *something* of what was contained in the claim: 'I decided to dive.'

Our claim then is that the phrase 'first cause' has such a complex logical structure as I have indicated. First, it is understood with reference to a situation which is evoked by developing the 'cause' model in the particular way which the qualifier 'first' suggests. The phrase then gives to the word 'God' a certain logical placing. The word 'God' is placed 'first' at the head of all causal stories, presiding over and uniting all causal explanations. Otherwise expressed, the word 'God' 'completes', and is logically prior to, all causal stories in the sense I have tried to illustrate by means of the swimming pool example. 'God' works something like the tautology 'I'm I'.

Let us now notice how, on this interpretation, we can avoid needless puzzles. Someone may object, for instance, that 'first cause' is nonsense. Does not the word 'cause' always imply a causal predecessor? We have 'proximate' cause, we have 'remote' cause, and these phrases are perfectly straightforward because 'cause' in each case implies causal predecessors either near or distant. But what can 'first cause' be if the word 'first' takes from 'cause' the very basis of its significance, namely that there should be causal predecessors? Is not 'first cause' self-contradictory?

On the basis of what we have said, the answer to this kind of objection is that, despite *grammatical* similarity, 'first cause' is not at all *logically* parallel to either 'proximate cause' or 'remote cause', but has rather the complex logical structure we have tried to show. The puzzle then disappears when the phrase is given the structure I have suggested. There is no reason whatever, especially at this time of the day, why we should wrestle with problems which have arisen from, or are perpetuated by, supposing that sentences which are similar in grammar have a similar logical structure.

2. *'Infinitely* WISE'

Let us see how this phrase can be given a structure very similar to that which we have just given to 'First Cause'.

Once again the word 'wise' names a model situation, and 'infinite' is a directive stimulating us to go on . . . and on . . . and on. . . . We might begin, for example, with the Third-Form boy who is 'scarcely wise', the Sixth-Form prefect who is 'rather wise'; the undergraduate 'definitely wise'; the lecturer (I should hope) 'very wise'; even wiser—well, the President of the Royal Society or the British Academy. So once again we continue to tell the story until the ice breaks; nor is there any risk of the story having to conclude at any particular point. For with regard to any idea of wisdom we have; with regard to any idea of wise person we know; it is always possible to think of a greater wisdom, or a person even wiser than that. It is, in other words, bound up with the very idea of 'wisdom' that no matter how wise a person is, he can always know a little more with profit. So, as I say, the story can go on for any length, and our hope is that at some point or other the ice will break, the light dawn, and a characteristically theological situation be evoked.

At this point, as before, the qualifier 'infinite' has now a second function. It claims for 'God' a distinctive logical placing, a presidential position over the whole language route. 'God' stands to the whole of whatever languages express wisdom—all the languages of discursive knowledge—something like a mathematical bound presides over, gathers together, and completes a sequence. So does the phrase 'infinitely wise' tell us how to use the word 'God' in relation to a situation we have called characteristically religious. Here is the kind of background against which people have spoken of 'wisdom' as a 'gift of God'. Here is the situation which the 'Wisdom' of Proverbs, Ecclesiasticus and the Wisdom Literature of the Old Testament presupposes. It may be that the 'fear of the Lord' is logically the 'beginning of wisdom', but it is, as a matter of psychological fact, only evoked at the *end* of a wisdom route.

In a similar way we may elucidate the phrase 'infinitely good', and this I will do before venturing two mathematical examples which will, I hope, make clearer something of what is involved in the procedure which I am commending for the better understanding of these theological phrases.

3. *'Infinitely* GOOD'

When we speak of God in terms of 'infinite goodness' it might seem as though we were making God the last term of a sequence such as the following:

Ferdinand Lopez	who is hardly good
Long John Silver	who is fairly good
Solomon	who was just good
David	who was very good
St Barnabas	who was very good indeed
St Francis	who was intensely good

. . . .
. . . .

then: God   who is infinitely good

It might seem as though, like the schoolmaster faced with his terminal reports, the theologian had a series of labels by which to classify the moral goodness he observes around him. All these labels except one, he may from time to time be found using for this or that Tom, Dick or Harry. The one exception is 'infinitely good'. This he reserves for God, who in various ways is somewhat exceptional. Here in outline is the ordinary picture, the picture the man in the street has of what the theologian is about, but with it come the well-known difficulties which the philosopher can only too easily raise when he shares with his comrade in the street this picture of the theological game. 'Good' (he will tell us) always implies 'better'. But those who talk of 'infinitely good' imply that we cannot go any further, that 'infinite good' is a good beyond which there is no better. But if so, 'infinitely good' is a meaningless phrase. In other words, the philosopher might say, by qualifying 'good' with 'infinitely', we have drained it of all the meaning it ever had, and we finish with an empirical void.

But those and similar difficulties are overcome if the ordinary picture does not give a true account of the theological game. What if this ordinary picture is logically misleading? What if 'infinite goodness' does not work at all like that? From what has been said already, it will come as no surprise to the reader to be told that the logical structure of the phrase 'infinite goodness' is something much more complex than the naïve use of the series of examples would

67

suggest. The theologian is not at all like the schoolmaster with his terminal reports. 'Infinitely good' is to be given the same kind of logical structure as 'infinitely wise'.

Once again we take goodness as a model—a word which gives us at once some picture of good behaviour, of a good man. In other words, there immediately comes to mind a member of such a series as we have mentioned above.

The first logical function of the word 'infinite' is to stimulate us to develop these 'stories of good lives' in the right direction. But in tracing such a sequence there is no intention of arriving at 'God' as a last term; the intention is to continue long enough with the sequence to evoke a situation characteristically different from the terms which preceded it; until we have evoked a situation not just characterized by a goodness which we admire or feel stirred to follow, but a situation in relation to which we are prepared to yield everything, 'soul, life and all'. Such a situation (as we saw at the end of Chapter I) is often labelled by the word 'Love', but only when 'Love' has a significantly odd behaviour. For here is adoration, wonder, worship, commitment. 'Love so amazing, so divine, demands my soul, my life, my all.'

Now at this point 'infinite' has a second logical function. We have already noticed the logical strain and impropriety —the 'difficulty'—of the phrase 'infinite goodness', and this impropriety reminds us that the phrase, while having such a basis as we have indicated in ordinary language, points to something outside 'good' language altogether. In this way it gives an appropriate placing to the word 'God'.

'Infinite', then, in these two ways qualifies the model 'good' and as so used 'infinite', like 'first' in 'first cause', is what we may call a logical qualifier—developing models in a useful direction, and pleading in the end an appropriate logical status for the word 'God'.

We may now notice that as qualifying models in theological phrases—'infinitely wise', or 'infinitely good'—the word 'infinite' has a logical behaviour closely akin to that which it possesses in mathematics. Let me illustrate this contention by two examples.

We may take as a first example a succession of regular polygons; triangle, square, pentagon, hexagon. . . . 3, 4, 5, 6 sides and so on. . . . What now of a regular polygon with an 'infinite number' of sides? Here is a directive to continue the sequence of regular polygons indefinitely. No matter how many sides we specify, the word 'infinite' tells us not to be content but to specify a regular polygon with at least one side more. So the succession of regular polygons could go on. To what purpose? If we increased the sides without limit, but kept the area approximately constant, there may suddenly dawn on us at a certain point the outline of something quite different: a circle. At this point there would be evoked what we might call 'mathematical insight'—something akin to the disclosure of a characteristically religious situation.

'Infinite' now has, as in the theological parallel, a second logical function. It can remind us that the word 'circle' commended in relation to this 'insight', has a logical behaviour very different from the phrase 'regular polygon'. Once again we might say that the very strain, the very impropriety, the 'difficulty' of talking about a regular polygon with an 'infinite number of sides' makes it plain that the word 'circle' is nothing if not logically odd from the standpoint of polygon language. The parallel with the theological case is plain.

As a second example we might return to our old friend, the succession of sums we have already mentioned: $1, 1 + \frac{1}{2}$,

$$1 + \frac{1}{2} + \frac{1}{2^2}, 1 + \frac{1}{2} + \frac{1}{2^2} + \frac{1}{2^3}, \cdot\cdot \ 1 + \frac{1}{2} + \frac{1}{2^2} \cdots \frac{1}{2^{n-1}}.$$

What now of the phrase 'infinite sum'? Parallel to the theological case we may say that the word 'sum' is a model and 'infinite' a qualifier, telling us in this case to expand the sums without limit. If someone mentions a sum with a million terms, expand it to have a million and one! So the phrase 'infinite sum' directs us to continue expanding our sums in this way.

Now, as with the series of 'good' lives, there may at a certain point be a 'disclosure', a characteristically different situation —what we may call mathematical insight—and in the mathematical case there might at the same time come to our minds the number '2'. But if we said that '2' was the 'infinite sum'—and it is certainly a number which no particular sum, however numerous its terms, will exceed—we can only mean that '2' is a number outside the series and of a different logical status altogether from the terms of the series, but a number which might be said to preside over and label the whole sequence of ever expanding sums.

'Infinite' then, as a theologian would use it, is not at all unlike its use in mathematics in relation to generated sequences for which a word of odd logic is posited at the end in relation to what could be called 'mathematical insight'. 'Infinite goodness' has a structure not all that unlike 'infinite sum' or 'infinite polygon', and if we wish to have some clues as to the logical placing of the word 'God', we may be helped by reflecting on the relation between 'circle' and the polygon stories, or '2' and the sequence stories.

Just as no polygon, however numerous its sides, is a circle; just as the sum of no series, however many its terms, is precisely 2; so God as 'infinitely good' is not on all fours with Long John Silver or even St Barnabas. 'Infinitely good' does not work at all like 'intensely good', let alone 'hardly good'. Hence such a question as: 'Since God is good and wise can he not, if these words have their normal meaning, be then somewhat better and wiser?' is a pseudo-question. It only arises if we have blundered in the logical placing of God. Or again, if it be said that 'infinite' drains from 'good' and 'wise' all the empirical relevance they ever had, our answer must be to show that 'infinite' does not qualify 'good' and 'wise' in this way, but is rather a logical qualifier developing a model in a certain direction.

4. 'CREATION *ex nihilo*'

How are we to understand this phrase? Is it the nonsense that some people have suggested? How could there be a 'nothing', they have objected, out of which something was created? Or again (it has been asked) what kind of basis in empirical fact could such a phrase ever have, since when there was merely 'nihil' there could plainly be nothing capable of empirical verification? Only when the process of 'creation *ex nihilo*' was completed could there be anything empirically significant to say about anything.

Presented with such problems, the first and indispensable step towards any kind of solution is to be clear what logical structure is being given to the phrase 'creation *ex nihilo*'. Once again, I suggest that we have here a qualified model.

In this case 'creation' is a down-to-earth word, a 'model', a word having a plain straightforward use in relation to ordinary situations. We are out walking with our dog which belongs to no obvious breed, and the unkind friend asks: 'What is that *creature* you have on the lead?' We are at a mannequin parade and the dress designer commends a 'magnificent *creation* from brocade'. The response he expects is 'How admirable, how unequalled, how perfect the design.' He hopes that, to use the familiar words, we shall be 'lost in wonder, love and praise'. Or we say of a notable painting, a poem, or some symphony, that it is an artistic, poetic, or musical *creation*.

Now it will be noticed at once that there is, *prima facie*, a difference between the case of the dog and the other cases we have taken. In the case of the dog there is a certain puzzlement and no more; here seems to be an odd phenomenon on the face of the earth, an unusual spatio-temporal pattern; something we have not seen the likes of before. But there is no wonder, no awe. In the other cases, however, there is something mysterious, something impressive, something, as we would say, which 'takes the breath away'; something which fills us with wonder, awe, astonishment. Of the evening dress, the picture, the poem, the symphony, we use appropriately odd phrases: We say, for example, that they exhibit a 'touch of genius'. We begin to use words like 'inspired' and so on. In short, in the second group of cases, there are parallels to the examples in our first chapter; there is in each case a 'discernment'; a situation has taken on depth; something is exhibited which is characteristically personal. There is a situation which exceeds what is seen, touched, heard, and so on, and which needs language appropriately odd by observational standards to describe it. But it is not necessarily *theological*. In other words, this situation of 'discernment' is not in *all* respects like those situations to which we appeal when *theological* words are used, though (like our earlier examples) it points towards them. We are still with our model; a particular poem, a work of art, a symphony. We are still in a world of poets, artists, musicians . . . we have not reached God. What we now have to do is to notice that in the case of the artist, the poet, and the musician, there is always dependence on pre-existing material; for example, the artistic 'creation' presupposes paint and brushes and the landscape; the poem demands a 'subject' and the medium in which it is exhibited; the musician needs his instrument, and it may be, his script; the dress designer his silk. So the second group of cases begins to concern itself with 'things' that occur on the surface of the earth . . . such as dogs. Now it is at this point that the qualifier '*ex nihilo*' comes to its own and begins to be useful. It may or may not be the case that our model situation has already exhibited wonder. The one possibility is exhibited by the poem, the work of art, the symphony; the other possibility is illustrated by the dog. But what must now happen is that in either case, and from 'things' such as paint, landscapes, musical instruments or dogs, a sense of wonder must be developed which has the whole universe as its focus. The technique which the qualifier '*ex nihilo*' recommends is that in all cases we should search for causal predecessors and go on searching . . . and searching . . . until once again the light breaks, and the penny drops, and we have in relation to the *whole universe* a 'wonderful situation' which could be called, and with significant impropriety, a 'sense of one-sided dependence'. In such a phrase we claim a certain similarity between that situation which breaks in on us in relation to the whole universe and that which broke in on us in the case of the evening dress, the picture, the poem, the symphony; cases where objects are dependent on their creators but not *vice versa*. But it has needed the qualifier *ex nihilo* to bring about cosmic discernment whether we start with a wonderful poem or a mongrel dog.

Now, once again, at this stage of cosmic discernment, the qualifier has a second function. This can be seen from the very strain, the very impropriety which *ex nihilo* gives to the phrase 'creation *ex nihilo*'. For in all the 'creation' stories we have told, there has always been *something* from which the 'creation' was effected; there have always been causal predecessors. So that 'creation' *ex nihilo* is on the face of it a scandal: and the point of the scandal is to insist that when the phrase has been given its appropriate empirical anchorage, any label, suited to that situation, must have a logical behaviour which, from the standpoint of down-to-earth 'creation' language, is odd. When creation *ex nihilo* as a qualified model evokes a characteristically religious situation —a sense of creaturely dependence—it further claims for the word 'God', which is then posited in relation to such a situation, that it caps all causal stories and presides over and 'completes' all the language of all created things. It places 'God' as a 'key' word for the universe of 'creatures'.

It is perhaps convenient to deal here with a question which might have been raised at many other points in the exposition. Is it not highly artificial and quite unsuited to a religious temperament (it might be said) to talk of positing the word 'God' in relation to a situation? Is this in fact what religious people do? The answer plainly is 'No'; but that is only to say that, regarded as a psychological account of religious belief, what we are giving now does not describe what always happens in the case of religious people. Nor would I claim that it does. All I claim is that it *could* happen, and, more importantly, it *must* happen if we want to show either the disbeliever, or the puzzled believer, what is the logical structure of religious phrases; if we wish to defend religious phrases against misunderstandings that can only too easily be raised against them.

If we are concerned, in other words, with the logical structure of the beliefs the religious man in fact has, there can be no objection to using language which talks of positing the word 'God'. In any event, what this language shows— and I think it is of general importance for the religious man to recognize the fact—is that theology is after all only *our* way of *talking* about God; and it will be noticed that I do *not* talk of positing *God*. What we posit is language which claims to talk about what is given and disclosed to us in a certain way.

In concluding this fourth example, let us now notice that once again various traditional puzzles are avoided if creation *ex nihilo* is given the kind of logical structure we have expounded above. If what we have said is right, '*ex nihilo*' is not a constructional phrase like 'in oils', or 'from stone', or 'from brocade'. To talk of a 'creation *ex nihilo*' is not at all like talking of a painting from oils, a building from stone, a dress from brocade. In other words, it is *not* something which can be the subject of a plain straightforward assertion. What we have been concerned to show is that, on the contrary, it

74

makes a very complex claim, but its claim is one which can nevertheless be defended in relation to certain empirical facts commended in a certain way. We may put the point alternatively by saying that whereas *creation ex nihilo* seems on the face of it, and from its grammar, to be talking of a great occasion in the past, it is rather making a present claim about God, and its logical grammar must be understood appropriately. The doctrine might perhaps be a little less misleading if it were expressed as 'creator *ex nihilo*', but then of course its connection with the world around us— with the 'creation'—would be somewhat unfortunately concealed.

When we would in all these ways emphasize the logical peculiarity of the phrase 'creation *ex nihilo*' let us in honesty confess that not all religious writers have always realized this point. As much as the irreligious, they have taken 'nothing' as equivalent to 'something'. For instance, Tillich speaks of the 'nihil out of which God creates' and Berdyaev tells us that 'out of the divine nothing God the Creator was born'. I do not say that these distinguished writers have no point to make when they talk this way, but I do say that their expression of it in such language is about as logically naïve and misleading as it possibly could be, and that any point as important as they are trying to make, deserves rather more careful formulation.

5. *'Eternal* PURPOSE'

Here again, a model-qualifier structure may be usefully given to this phrase. Indeed, purpose stories are pre-eminently those which make situations come alive, where we are caught up in wonder, where the light dawns. A purpose story is often very successful in bringing about 'discernment'. In this connection let Paley be given the justice which is his due, even though he may also deserve various criticisms.

Certainly we parody Paley if we represent him merely as

arguing: the world is like a watch; watches have makers; therefore the world has a maker—God. On the contrary, Paley has another point to make of considerable importance, though it is often overlooked. It is a point which is of permanent value even when critics like Hume have done their worst with any argument from analogy such as that we have just summarized. It may be seen in this way. Recall Paley's story of walking on a heath. His foot kicks against a stone. There is, here, no problem and no wonder. It never occurs to us to ask: 'How did this stone come to be there?' We are not 'astonished' that we find a stone. But suppose there happened to be not a stone but something like a watch on the ground. Then we ask a question, 'Why is this thus?' And as we pursue our examination, the watch seems 'wonderfully' intricate and purposive, and in the end we talk of a maker. But of course if watches were as common as stones, no question would be asked of the watch either. In other words, Paley is important as suggesting that we shall only take up a theological standpoint towards the universe if we have a questioning mind, which pursues its questions until there breaks in on us a situation which is characterized by depth, wonderment, and so on. The particular way of pursuing questions in order to reach this wonderment which Paley would specially commend is that which seeks after purposive connections, which asks in all cases for a 'purpose' in order to understand why such and such is the case. We may look at the universe, Paley would say, and it may seem to be no more than one thing knocking against another— feet hitting stones. But then perhaps with a watch in mind as a sort of model or catalyst, we may begin to seek for purposes where we had not discerned purpose before, and it is in pursuing such a purposive quest that the light may well dawn. Paley's claim is that if we look at the universe as *he* looked at the watch, the characteristic situation may be evoked. As Paley with his watch, so we may see intricate and fascinating connections in the universe; we may piece together what had before been separated, and what seems so flat, ordinary, straightforward, may well become 'wonderful', 'alive'. We are reminded of George Herbert's lines: 'Whoever looks on glass (and recollecting Paley's story we may add, or on a stone) on it may stay his eye (and bother no further), or if he pleaseth through it pass; and then the heavens espy'—when the light dawns, the penny drops, and there is 'discernment'.

Now it is in such a way as this that, starting with 'purpose' as our model—the 'purpose' which a watch may display— 'eternal' develops purpose stories. It tells us to prosecute them in such and such a direction until wonder is evoked; and when that occurs the very strain and impropriety of the phrase 'eternal purpose'—which sets alongside a temporal model of purpose a word like 'eternal' which seems to be nothing if not other than time—pleads a correct, and appropriately odd, logical placing for the word 'God'. The pattern of a watch may be purposive and witness straightforwardly to a maker. But we have only 'God' when purpose stories (which are so readily associated with wonder) have been developed in relation to the whole universe, when 'purpose' has been qualified in such a way as to make it evident that the word 'God', appropriate to the *cosmic* wonder which is evoked, is *not* a logical synonym of maker. Nor can we speak straightforwardly and without qualification of God's 'purpose'. This was the mistake Paley made. Paley, we might say, was in principle right about the kind of situation which would justify religious language, but when he labelled his situation of wonder, his language failed miserably to give an appropriately odd currency to the word 'God'. Ironically enough, Hume, in effect, shows how inadequately a watchmaker God fits into traditional theology; but Hume no more than Paley does justice to the 'feeling' of purposiveness evoked by the universe. 'Tell me, from your own feeling, if

77

the idea of a contriver does not immediately flow in upon you with a force like that of sensation.'[1] So says Hume through the mouth of Cleanthes. Here is a 'sense' of purpose —a discernment—which both Paley and Hume admit, but for which neither of them finds logically appropriate language. Neither the watchmaker of Paley, nor the merely negative contribution of Hume, is very impressive.

Differing from both, we must insist on the complex logical structure of the phrase 'eternal purpose'. Once again we may remark that to do this is to avoid certain other puzzles and difficulties. For instance, it has often been said that purpose is the last stronghold of anthropomorphism. Did not John Stuart Mill say that the more we were justified in talking of God's purpose, the more we would have to deny his omnipotence, since purpose involves the following of a plan, it implies a struggle against difficulties. 'Purpose' seems to be something belonging essentially to our own finitude. But all these difficulties we can readily admit without anxiety when we recognize that purpose is nothing but a *model* when used of God, a *model* which has to be qualified before it is suitable currency, and which *is* qualified by the word 'eternal', as it might be also by such a word as 'inscrutable' or 'infinite'. It is because of such qualifiers, and only when he is careful never to overlook such qualifiers, that the theist can listen undeterred to the charge of anthropomorphism.

Again, what we have said can help to meet the objection that 'eternal purpose' is self-contradictory. We can readily admit that there is a logical strain or impropriety about the phrase, which arises by bringing alongside the word 'purpose' such a word as 'eternal'. We can also admit that if 'eternal' qualified 'purpose' in a straightforward way so that 'eternal purpose' was a logical kinsman of 'broad purpose'

---

[1] *Dialogues Concerning Natural Religion*, Part III, (Kemp Smith edition, p. 191).

or 'limited purpose' or 'short-lived purpose', the phrase would certainly be self-contradictory. But despite appearances, despite grammatical similarities, 'eternal purpose' has (as we have tried to show) a very different logical structure from these other phrases. Watchmakers have often a limited purpose; Managing Directors have often broad purposes; politicians, short-lived purposes, but when we talk of 'eternal purpose' it is important to remember that we are using a phrase whose logical behaviour must match up to the logical oddity which is 'God'. If we suppose 'eternal purpose' to be a self-contradictory phrase, we are mistakenly assimilating God to a watchmaker, a Managing Director, or a politician.

There then is an outline of the logical behaviour of some of the words and phrases that are used about God, and I would like to emphasize three points in relation to the whole discussion.

(a) Whether the light breaks or not is something that we ourselves cannot entirely control. We can certainly choose what seem to us the most appropriate models, we can operate what seem to us the most suitable qualifiers; we can develop what seem to us the best stories, but we can never guarantee that for a particular person the light will dawn at a particular point, or for that matter at any point in any story. Need this trouble us? Is not this only what has been meant by religious people when they have claimed that the 'initiative' in any 'disclosure' or 'revelation' must come from God? It would certainly not accord with what religious people have claimed if we could take some particular model, develop it with some particular qualifier, and produce God. That would be semantic magic. Nor if we could develop some particular story could we guarantee God's emergence. For we should then have a technique which gave us power over God. The religious person must always assert that there can be no formula guaranteed to produce God for inspection.

79

(b) On the other hand, we must recognize that while some people are impervious to some models and qualifiers, to some routes and to some stories, they may not be to others. The characteristic situation may be evoked for some by telling causal stories, for others by telling wisdom stories, for others by telling stories of good lives, for others by telling creation stories, for others by telling purpose stories. In fact there is no word which, in principle, cannot lead to a story which might evoke the characteristic situation in which God is known. This is only saying of course, in another way, that in principle God may be discovered at every point in his creation.

(c) We have already seen how various difficulties and misunderstandings are avoided once a particular logical structure is given to certain theological phrases—difficulties and misunderstandings which are otherwise bound to arise, and which can seriously hinder apologetic.

I would like to illustrate this point further by reference to another problem, and some would say that for the believer it is the major problem—the problem of evil. I shall not in any way attempt a full treatment of the problem. I merely hope to illustrate, by reference to this problem, the kind of logical moves that have been evolved in some of the traditional discussions of it.

In the first place, let us see how *a* problem of evil arises directly from our discussion of models and qualifiers. It has been part of my main thesis that any word may be a 'model' by means of which a characteristically religious situation can be evoked. All words, if suitably qualified, can lead to such a situation; and this, as we have just said above, is equivalent to the Christian claim that God can be seen in all the words of his creation. But, it might be said, can *all* words be so used? What in particular of the word 'evil'? Can we talk of God in terms of 'infinitely evil', precisely as we have talked about him in terms of 'infinitely good'?

Now I think we are bound to agree that in principle the word 'evil' might be used as a model for producing situations which are 'awful' and 'mysterious'. We may recall the 'awful' symmetry of Blake's tiger as he presents himself to us in a ravenous mood in the forest at night. But when from the word 'evil' a characteristically religious situation has been produced, religious people have generally posited in relation to such a situation, not the word 'God', but the word 'devil'. Here indeed would be the logic of the word 'devil', and I do not deny that it has a logical placing very similar to that of 'God'. But this now means that we have *prima facie* two key words: what has been traditionally called a 'dualism'. Our religious commitment, expressed in terms of God, can no longer claim to be a *total* loyalty to the *whole* universe. In this way, there arises from our discussion a 'problem' of evil.

With this approach, let us now look at the logical moves which have characterized four traditional ways of dealing with the problem.

(a) One way of re-creating a unified picture—and avoiding the dualism—has been to relate the two provisional key words 'God' and 'devil' by the story of 'The Fall', and having unified the two language schemes in this way, to have as a final picture *one* key word 'God' logically prior to 'The Fall'. In this way a story (of the Fall) has been developed to resolve the difficulty of two key words, to relate consistently 'God' and 'devil'. The story of the Fall may thus be seen as a straining after consistency, as an enterprising attempt to secure consistent talking at the second move.

Meanwhile, let us notice that if stories of the Fall have this logical function, if they provide consistency links between diverse language maps, then 'the Fall' is a logical *rara avis*, a curiosity indeed. Whatever the phrase 'The Fall' does or does not refer to, it should be quite plain that its logic is *not* that of observational language. 'The Fall' can describe no 'going-on' backstage before the cosmic drama began; if we talk of it as 'pre-mundane' let us not imply that it was something going on behind the scenes before the mundane play started. To talk of the Fall as 'pre-mundane' is best understood by changing in the first place to the formal mode, that is by interpreting the claim in terms of language. 'The Fall was pre-mundane' can be taken as saying that 'The Fall' does not belong to 'mundane language', but is something or other which all mundane language presupposes. So the doctrine of the Fall is first and foremost consistency-language, and if we ask after its empirical anchorage, our answer must be that this can and must be found only in the kind of situation which justifies our talk about God.

Let us not suppose that any and every theological word describes a separate feature of the supernatural scene. Theological language can be made significant and empirically grounded without its nouns having to talk of particular landmarks in the way they would do if it was ordinary matter-of-fact language. Indeed, the curse of much theological apologetic is that it talks as if theological language worked like ordinary matter-of-fact language, which is precisely what his opponents wish to hear the theologian say, for then theology has lost the day before the battle begins. The Fall is a particular case in point.

(b) But there have been other ways of meeting the problem of evil, and the second kind of move we must consider distinguishes between God as 'permitting', and God as 'willing' evil. In other words, to avoid a dualism, 'evil' is linked with 'God' by the word 'permit'.

So our second way of attacking the problem of evil begins with the human distinction between deliberate 'willing' and 'permitting'. The Chairman of the British Transport Commission may will a special train to take members of the Commission to inspect the new restaurant (say) at Crewe; he may be said also to will the general pattern of British

Railways. But we could not say that he wills that the local train from Banbury to Woodford Halse should leave just as the train from Oxford to Banbury approaches Banbury Station, so causing loss of tempers and connections for many passengers. We might say that he 'permits' this, since it is something under his general control and something he could alter but which he refrains from changing because (he might say) he wishes to teach greater determination and self-reliance to the drivers of Oxford engines. If they knew that Sir Brian Robertson would adjust their time schedule to suit whenever they failed to keep time, they would themselves never learn to run the trains efficiently between Oxford and Banbury. So to teach the Oxford engine drivers keenness and determination, the Chairman of the British Transport Commission 'permits' time-tables to be misleading, and passengers to lose their connections at Banbury, though he does not 'will' these distressing occasions. So much for other kinds of story which predicate 'permitting' and 'willing' of one person. Now such a story, or one very like it, is used as a way of talking about God both in relation to good and evil: God 'wills' the good, but 'permits' the evil. 'Evil' is linked to the one word 'God' in virtue of the word 'permitting'; 'good', by the word 'willing'.

But of course this integration of 'good' and 'evil' into one language is only justified if we can also speak of some particular 'purpose' on God's part to compare with that we have attributed to Sir Brian Robertson in the development of the story. Theologians then are rightly consistent when, in distinguishing between God's willing and permitting evil, they add that this is done for a special purpose, namely to create a harmonious community of free human beings who have learnt responsibility, self-reliance and so forth.

It might well be felt, however, at this point that the God we now have is far too much like the Chairman of the British Transport Commission to be the kind of God in

83

which religious people would believe, and this reminds us that all we have done in relation to the problem of evil is to produce a language-map by which the dualism can be avoided. The next possible move would be to qualify such a purpose model as the map involves, with a word like 'eternal' in the way we have already hinted earlier in the chapter, so that the whole map finds its empirical sanction in an appropriately religious situation.

Of course there are alternative stories which might hold together the distinction between permitting and willing, in the way we have seen that purpose stories do. Two of the most common alternatives to purpose stories have been those which have spoken of 'limitation' or 'condescension'— which have used these models in preference to one of purpose. It is as if Sir Brian Robertson, for example, had wisely and judiciously limited himself to certain activities, knowing full well that he could not attend to every detail perfectly. Or he might well—for the sake of brotherly feeling towards the engine drivers—'condescend' to work on the footplate himself without giving explicit suggestions to drivers as to how their driving could be improved. But once again, if we are to build on the distinction between permitting and willing in a way that is appropriate to God, these alternative models of 'limitation' and 'condescension' must in their turn be qualified. Hence theologians have traditionally spoken of God's 'self-limitation' or his 'infinite condescension'. It is important that we realize what the logical pattern of such phrases is, and in particular we must *not* take them as belonging to the descriptive psychology of God. Rather are they once again, and like much philosophical theology and Christian doctrine, rules for our consistent talking. They do not straightforwardly describe God. Rather do they tell us how we must talk about God if we wish to reckon squarely with the evil in the Universe, and at the same time to talk of him consistently, and always in reference to such empirical

84

situations of 'wonder' and 'worship' as we consider through these chapters.

(c) We will now look at a third treatment of the problem of evil which involves logical moves of a somewhat different kind from those we have been considering so far. This solution endeavours to find some super-model in terms of which 'good' and 'evil' can, *here and now*, be put together in terms of a consistent story. Thereafter, we speak of God in terms of this super-model suitably qualified. Let us see in rather more detail how this kind of solution works. One super-model makes use of the fact that we need a constant background if we are to effect any moral training whatever. It is no use training our children to be punctual for school if we never know what time the classes will begin. More broadly, it is no use urging people to be benevolent, if the bread they are giving to the deserving turns to stone in hungry mouths: it is no use planning some generous behaviour if we have no sort of guarantee that tomorrow will be, broadly speaking, very much like today. But, the story goes, this constant background which is required for moral behaviour, also leads to disasters. If for the sake of morality our lives are lived in an environment constant enough to be characterized by general rules, these same rules may well lead to unfortunate results. For example, when spheres are cooling, since it is a general feature of the Universe that the outside cools quicker than the inside, then this must happen to the earth itself, and the consequent strains will produce earth cracks and tremors. But if there were not this general feature of the universe it would mean that all our food would only be cool enough to eat on the outside when the inside had become so cold as to be unbearable; and so on. So a super-model which talks about moral training, inevitably unites on the one hand features which are morally commendable, and on the other hand disastrous. Good and evil are brought together within a super-model which has our moral approbation.

85

There is another super-model which has this same theme of 'moral training', and once again unites good and evil here and now in a situation which commands our moral approval. It is pointed out, and truly, that if parents in their children, or schoolmasters in their pupils, wish to develop responsible personalities, there must be enough latitude given to behaviour for there to be a certain amount of wrong-doing—that this is the 'price to be paid' for responsible persons. If a person has this latitude, he will sometimes make a fool of himself; but the alternative is that, having no latitude whatever, the child will cease to be a person. Broadening the model, it is said that such evils of human conflict as war or jealousy may be seen as part of the price to be paid if we wish to effect at some time or another a harmonious community of freely responsible people. The two models we have just been considering, and specially the second, might be seen as special cases of what is called 'redeeming love'. The person who suffers undeservedly by our general rules, who suffers our 'indifferent' justice, is the person who specially merits our mercy, our active loving kindness. Again, it may be that the child who has been given freedom makes a fool of himself, but it is in relation to the prodigal that we are given one of our most impressive accounts of 'redeeming love'. Further, it would be claimed that if such a love is exercised, there will come out of the situation which seems temporarily disastrous, a personality better than the one which went into it. So we see how 'redeeming love' specifies situations where evil is overcome; situations moreover which are in the end all the better for having had the evil there, once this evil has been redeemed. 'Redeeming love' is yet another super-model which incorporates evil organically in a situation which is morally laudable.

Now, so far, there has been no reference whatever to God. So far no more than human situations have been considered and in this regard the example differs somewhat from the two earlier ones. But at this point these human situations in which good and evil are brought together in a morally praiseworthy manner, these situations which are most characteristically labelled 'redeeming love', are taken as situations in terms of which to model God. Once again the model must of course be qualified, for instance by such a word as 'supreme' or 'infinite'. So the problem of evil is resolved for the theist in this third case if he is able to speak of God in terms of 'supreme redeeming love'.

Two points as corollaries:

(i) Taking our last remarks with what was said much earlier, it is plain that such a solution to the problem of evil as we have outlined, brings with it as *a logical necessity* a total commitment to the Universe. If we speak of God in terms of 'supreme redeeming love', there must go with that the response of 'soul, life, and all'. Thus, properly speaking, the problem of evil is only 'solved' when we have not only formulated a consistent way of talking, but when that way of talking brings with it a commitment to the Universe which, as part of itself and in particular, struggles with and overcomes the evil from which the problem began.

(ii) But once again let it be emphasized that when we speak of God in terms of 'supreme redeeming love' we are not making an assertion in descriptive psychology— we are not claiming to know something about the private life of God. If we speak of God in terms of 'redeeming love' we are using a model, and to be suitable currency for God the model must be qualified, whereupon the resultant phrase has a complex logical structure and one which is only to be understood in relation to such a situation as we discussed in the first chapter.

(d) At this point, the reader may well express his surprise that no account has yet been taken of the Hebrew assertion that God is 'author of good and evil' alike. What do we make of this bold claim to place 'God' as well by such a phrase as 'infinitely evil', as by 'infinitely good'? If we are not to misunderstand it, however, we must above all remind ourselves how conscious the Hebrews were of the *transcendence* of God. They were nothing if not emphatic that 'God' was a word *outside* ordinary language. In other words, they were so sure of the logical distance between 'God' and both 'good' and 'evil', that they were not likely to misunderstand such a phrase as 'author of good and evil'. Indeed, the word 'author' acts something like a qualifier in doing justice to all the transcendence that the characteristically religious situation gave to them. For let us notice that from 'God is the author of good and evil' it does *not* follow that we can say significantly 'God is good' or 'God is evil'. As the Hebrews were never likely to think that God was just 'good', no more were they likely to think of him as just 'evil', and 'author' represented to them mystery and awe. Hence the Hebrews found no difficulty in linking 'God' *in this way* with both 'good' and 'evil'. They were saved from any likely misunderstanding by their sense of God's transcendence. Contrariwise, we might well think that our own troubles about evil have arisen because we have lost what once they had: and because only too often do we think our models—be they 'good' or 'evil'—represent God without qualification. Our troubles with God and evil often arise because we have spoken too easily, and too casually of God as 'good'.

Finally, what we have said will, I hope, do something to illuminate yet another problem—the old problem of having to speak of God as both being 'loving' and 'impassible'. If 'God is impassible' and 'God is loving' have the same logical structure; if they each say the same sort of thing in the same sort of way about God, then it is impossible to escape from the antinomy they present. But the considerations we have developed in this chapter help us to see how this apparent antinomy can be resolved. The two assertions have each a different logical structure and their claims are not at all incompatible.

We have seen that *'God is impassible'*, like 'God is immutable', is to be understood by its ability to evoke in terms of
'passibility' stories what we have called the characterististic
theological situation. Further, when the light dawns and
the penny drops, to say that 'God is impassible' is to claim
that the word 'God' is a word which cannot be confined to
passibility language. In other words, this first assertion con-
centrates on evoking the fact and claiming that the word
'God' is nothing if not logically odd.

We saw earlier that the other assertion: *'God is loving'*
claims that we can model God in terms of 'loving' situations;
but we also saw that, as it stands, the assertion is logically
incomplete in an important way, and that to avoid this in-
completion we ought to insert some appropriate qualifier
such as 'infinitely' or 'all'. More correctly, then, we must
say: 'God is infinitely loving', or 'God is all-loving' when we
have a qualified model of the kind we have been discussing
in Section III of this chapter. It is now plain that as containing a model qualified in this way, this second assertion has a
different logical structure from 'God is impassible'. Each
assertion evokes the suitably odd situation, each claims an
odd positioning for the word 'God', a position away from the
straightforward language of passibility or love; but the
second assertion is more positive in claiming that this special
positioning can nevertheless be reached from ordinary
language, to which words like 'love' belong, once this
ordinary language has been appropriately qualified, as by
the word 'infinite'.

Here then is a method by which not only are problems
overcome, but where at every point we plot and map our
theological phrases with reference to a characteristically
religious situation—one of worship, wonder, awe. Without
such an empirical anchorage all our theological thinking is
in vain, and where there is controversy and argument we are
to look for their resolution where they are fulfilled: in worship.

III

CHRISTIAN LANGUAGE

I. THE LANGUAGE OF THE BIBLE

IN previous chapters I have been urging that religious language has to be logically odd to be appropriate currency for such an odd situation as religious people claim to speak about. Here (as we saw in Chapter I) is a discernment which provokes a commitment; a claim to which a religious man makes an appropriate response. Here is a discernment which is perceptual and more; whereupon situations become distinctively different, a difference we have tried to describe by speaking of the light dawning, the ice breaking, the penny dropping. Further, when such a discernment occurs, it provokes (we saw) a total commitment to what is discerned; we yield ourselves in religious loyalties as conscience yields to the claims of duty, and our religious devotion has similarities to that devotion which we show to persons, communities and nations.

Against this kind of background we tried, in Chapter II, to elucidate in some detail the logical behaviour of various words and phrases used about God. Far from talk about divine attributes being logically straightforward, we could distinguish at least three logical areas within it. First there were the attributes such as 'immutability', 'impassibility', whose main function was to evoke the characteristically religious situation, though such attributes did also plead negatively the distance of the word 'God' from observational language. There were then those attributes such as 'unity' and 'simplicity', whose function was once again to evoke the discernment-commitment, though this time they made a rather more positive language claim in relation to it. Such attributes (we saw) claimed a key position for the word 'God' in relation to all other categories. Thirdly, with respect to such phrases as 'first cause', 'infinite wisdom', 'creation *ex nihilo*', 'eternal purpose', we saw how each of these had the logical structure of a qualified model, where the qualifier had a two-fold function. First, it developed 'model' stories in a particular direction until the typically religious situation was evoked. Thereupon, in the second place, it claimed an appropriately odd logical position for the word 'God'. At various points in the chapter, and again at the end, we saw how traditional puzzles and problems could be illuminated, and the logical significance of various theological claims made clearer, if we were prepared to give to theological language the oddness which is its legitimate due. The overall moral was: Let us always be cautious of talking about God in straightforward language. Let us never talk as if we had privileged access to the diaries of God's private life, or expert insight into his descriptive psychology so that we say quite cheerfully why God did what, when and where.

In all these ways, then, I have been urging that religious language is odd. But, it may be retorted: what of the language of the Bible? Is this logically odd? On the contrary, is it not very straightforward? Is not the Bible, then, an exception to what I have been saying? In this chapter I shall try to argue, however, that the language of the Bible is appropriately odd, too; a view which I hope to support with illustrations. But we had better clear away a difficulty at the start.

Because (or so I would urge) the language of the Bible has an appropriately odd logical structure, I do *not* imply that it was consciously constructed in this way by its writers, any more than I would believe that, generally speaking, a poet works explicitly according to a formal pattern in writing a poem. They wrote; nay more, they were inspired; they could not help therefore giving their language an odd structure if it was to be appropriate currency for their significant situations. But this is *not* to say that they were semantically-minded, and strove deliberately to construct their phrases according to some conscious logical plan. A parallel with mathematics may help.

For centuries people did arithmetic in school, home and market place, and asked no questions about its logical structure. A man selling carpets at the market cared nothing for axiomatic systems. 'Your room is 9 sq. yds., madam, and square? You want a piece 3×3.' No difficulty! But supposing a wag shouts from the crowd: 'What about my room, mister? Minus 9 sq. yds.' What does the salesman do about the square root of -9? Why is he now incompetent, whereas on the previous occasion the sale proceeded without interruption? If $\sqrt{9}$ is straightforward, why does $\sqrt{-9}$ puzzle us? It was to meet certain puzzles—of which that is a travesty—that people began to look for the first time at the logical structure of arithmetic; that they began to ask, for the first time, what logical account could be given of arithmetic, algebra and the rest, when they do the job they are meant to do? Further, it was asked, can we offer any consistent development of this logical structure which might enable us to meet this new difficulty about negative quantities? And so on. No one would suggest that to do arithmetic everyone must *consciously* move according to the pattern of a recognized axiomatic system; but if and when we come across difficulties of an intractable kind, such difficulties demand that we look into the logical pattern which our arithmetical behaviour has in fact had, though we have never hitherto explicitly recognized it.

The same is true of the Bible. Those who wrote the books must (if I am right) and simply because they were inspired, have written in a manner which in fact is logically odd. But this does *not* mean that self-consciously, and deliberately, they constructed their phrases to certain logical patterns. Further, I agree that we need not bother about the logical structure of Bible-language until difficulties arise. But these difficulties are now with us. What are they? They are difficulties raised by such questions as: What is the Bible about? What are the Gospels about? What kind of 'fact' does the Bible in general, the Gospels in particular, describe? Questions are being raised on all sides about myth, typology, and so on, and it is such topics which raise explicitly questions about the logical structure of Bible-language.

PART I. SOME GENERAL REFLECTIONS

To justify that contention; to see both the difficulties which have arisen and their philosophical character, let us look in the first part of this chapter at the broad historical background. We may usefully begin with John Locke, for whom the Bible was 'plain and intelligible', setting forth the truths of the Christian religion in a manner suited to those who had neither time, nor interest, nor ability to follow abstruse arguments. In Locke's own words, the Bible gave religion 'to those whose hand is used to the plough, to say nothing of the other sex'.[1] Now of course it is true that simple people have understood the Bible as well as the most distinguished theologians. We may even say that sometimes they have understood it better, because as the theologian himself would be the first to admit, his thorn in the flesh, his occupational disease, is that his very preoccupation with theology may atrophy his vision. At any rate Locke's view has this truth in it—that what the Bible is about is something which the simplest can know as well as the expert. But that is still *not* to say that the *logical structure* of the Bible is 'plain' and 'straightforward', unless we make the mistake of supposing that a language which is grammatically simple, or in

[1] *The Reasonableness of Christianity, as delivered in the Scriptures.*

93

some other way psychologically assimilable, has a straight-forward logic. If the recent preoccupations of philosophy with language tell us anything, they should warn us emphatically against making that particular mistake. Whatever the Bible is about, it must make its point to the simplest person—that is taken for granted by all Christians. But does it follow that the language of the Bible is *logically* simple and straightforward? Is its topic simple?

People have so often assumed affirmative answers to these questions. When the 'plainest', 'unambiguous', and most 'straightforward' language seemed to be science, there were many who claimed that the language of the Bible was scientific, and there began the era of what can be alternatively described as 'scientific' or 'historical' criticism, for it was one of the assumptions of the day that 'history was science, neither more nor less'. The movement was paralleled in philosophy by the search for a perfect language, a language which should be free from all ambiguity and in no way misleading. The quest for the historical Jesus was the theological counterpart of Russell's quest for unambiguous uses. Russell believed that his quest had succeeded with the discovery of what he called 'sense data', which could lead to 'atomic propositions' which in a complex build-up could give rise to all the compound sentences of ordinary language. In like manner it was supposed that the languages of history and theology were scientific in structure and appealed in the end to 'sense data': what could be seen, touched, tasted, and so on.

This was, for instance, the era of Sir John Hawkins' *Horae Synopticae*, when people analysed the Gospels into groups of verses, and counted recurrent words just as they would analyse chemical compounds into various elements or count lead pellets. Over all lay a statistical interest, and an echo of Russell's ideal of a scientific language can be seen for instance in the titles which Sir John Hawkins gives to various sections of Part III of his book. For instance, he speaks of 'passages which may have been omitted or altered as being liable to be misunderstood, or to give offence, or to suggest difficulties'.[1] Now if we had before us the ideal of a perfectly unambiguous language, this would be an appropriate sentiment, for it assumes that 'odd' passages are of no value, and that the narrative gains by their omission. If we could assume the Gospel writers had Russell's ideal in mind, that would be a fair assumption; but my contrary claim would be that 'oddness' deserves a second look. It *may* be misleading or valueless, but it can be revealing instead—a possibility for which Russell made no allowance.

Again, in the title of another section there is reference to: 'enlargements of the narrative which add nothing to the information conveyed by it because they are expressed again or are directly involved in the Context'.[2] Once again we have the ideal of a scientific language. There is no point, Hawkins would say, in having p twice. Anything which is 'expressed again' will 'add nothing to the information' we have already been given. That of course is very true, but it assumes that the purpose of the Gospels is 'to give us information', and it is this assumption we would question. An example may illustrate the point I have in mind: as we travel along a certain road we find repeated at intervals of 100 yards signs which say: 'Road Works Ahead'. Plainly, except in ways which at the moment are irrelevant, any later notice gives us no more 'information' than did the earlier one, and if we all acted with admirable scientific precision, one notice should suffice, and so sometimes it does. Nor need the repetition of the signs merely be done as a safety device in case we chance to miss one or more. The contractor may wish to impress on us what might be called the 'degree' of danger. He may wish to make sure that an *authoritative* warning is given to us, a challenge of the order he intends, a

[1] J. C. Hawkins: *Horae Synopticae*, O.U.P., 1909, Pt. IIIA., Section I.
[2] Loc. cit., Pt. IIIA, Section II.

challenge to which we will give an appropriate response. To effect this purpose he repeats his 'information'. So let it never be supposed that what is said twice is no more significant than what is said once. Repetition may be by no means logically superfluous—though admittedly in a scientific context it would be.

Finally, let us recall the title of one more section of Hawkins' book: 'Rude, harsh, obscure or unusual words or expressions which may therefore have been omitted or re-placed by others.'[1] It is true that Hawkins very wisely says only that these '*may* have been omitted or replaced'. But this very possibility is enough to make my point. The interest-ing point is that, for Hawkins at any rate, *if* they had been so replaced, there would have been no loss, but on the contrary, a gain. 'Rude, harsh, obscure, or unusual words or expressions' could have no telling point. But that, it will be seen, is precisely the opposite of what we are claiming in this book. What we would now claim, indeed, is that unless the language of the Gospels is logically odd, it will not tell of the kind of situation which can be properly called 'religious'.

But Hawkins was not alone in his contentions. We had what were called synoptic 'hypotheses' which used symbols such as $M_1 M_2 M_3$, and talked of protoluke as though it were logically not very much unlike parabenzene. It is not my point here to show how such synoptic hypotheses were always very much unlike scientific hypotheses, and that in particular their advocates never distinguished between the probabilifying of a hypothesis and its consistent expansion. All I am concerned to show at the moment is that the whole approach to theological language was meant to be scientific. Nor do I wish to poke fun at this approach and intention. For those who were scientific-minded, and for those—and they were very many—for whom science spelled wonder and awe, the main weakness and one which belongs to this

[1] Loc. cit., Pt. IIIA, Section IV.

approach in principle, is that from the Christian standpoint it can allow nothing distinctive about the Bible. The Bible could talk of God no better than—though it is only fair to say no worse than—a scientific text book could. Not only was the Bible like any other book; it was particularly like a text book of science. Further, let us recognize that, when biblical criticism was in full swing, there lay behind this scientific approach to the Bible the desire to establish biblical facts as incontrovertibly as those facts talked of by science. There was, in short, the desire to find, by means of science, a firm foundation in fact for a religion of the Bible.

But not only did this approach never succeed in producing a non-controversial historical Jesus; we have by this time seen that there is no single homogeneous scientific language; and we are at the present moment very puzzled as to what science is about. All we can be sure of is that it is *not* about isolable objective facts which we merely scan from a distance, like small boys at a fair watching the clay pipes, or Kelly's Wedding, going round and round the shooting booth. Yet it is not only for all these reasons that we now find great difficulties about a scientific approach to the Bible. There is an even more important difficulty. We have now come to see, by the development of biblical criticism itself, that the empirical anchorage of the Christian faith is not in the kind of situation with which *any* scientific language, as such, could adequately deal. To see how this conclusion has been reached we must proceed with our historical survey.

It was in a large measure the disappointment that a non-controversial historical Jesus never emerged from the methods of scientific criticism, that there arose a different approach to the Gospel language, motivated by a literary rather than a scientific interest, so that scientific-historical criticism gave place to 'form criticism'. Such an approach to the Gospels distinguished, for instance, 'miracle stories', 'apothegms', 'the words of Jesus', 'prophetic sayings', 'apocalyptic sayings', 'sayings about the law' and so on. Here was an attempt to understand the Gospels in terms of certain complex forms of literary appreciation. Now it was from seeking for the factual implications of this literary analysis that attention came more and more to be centred on history and the historical community of the Christian Church, where 'history' means something different from the 'history' which has hitherto been understood in a *scientific* sort of way. In brief, the literary forms were to be understood by reference to the Christian faith and life in which they had emerged; the Gospels had been produced out of a cultic motive. As the early Bultmann says in 'The Study of the Synoptic Gospels', translated by Frederick Grant and included in a book whose general title is *Form Criticism*, published in 1924:

'One may designate the final motive by which the gospels were produced as the *cultic* (that is, the needs of common worship), if one considers that the high point of Christian life was the gathering of the community for worship, when the figure of Jesus, his teaching as well as his life, was set forth before the eyes of the faithful, and when accordingly the gospels served for public reading.'

But as criticism developed, the results became inevitably more complex. It was not long before parallels were drawn between these literary forms used in the Gospel and what were common literary forms in the community around. Where then was the distinctiveness of Christianity? The outcome was that we may see emerging from form criticism, two positions—the one more conservative, the other less so. The more conservative reaction (A) was filled with a growing conviction that 'history' is a discipline all of its own, and claimed that the distinctiveness of the Bible is found in such history as this which is not at all scientific in character: a 'historical basis' which enables the Gospels to be distinguished sharply from other literary creations, e.g.

imaginative fiction. There was, on the other hand, a less conservative reaction (B) which endeavoured to find in existentialism parallels or clues to the odd facts which are the subject of the Gospel narratives, and in which the distinctiveness of Christianity is to be found. Let us look at these two reactions in turn: both are features of the contemporary scene.

(A) If we say that the Bible is about historical facts and give Queen Anne's death, and Caesar's crossing the Rubicon as examples of historical facts, the difficulty plainly arises: what is there distinctive about the 'facts' of the Bible? If in answer to that question we say that the 'facts' of the Bible are *not* 'just like' Queen Anne's death or Caesar's crossing the Rubicon, but are nevertheless 'history', then plainly we are using 'history' in a strange way. This, I think, is normally the position which is taken up on the first alternative. But is it a sufficient account of the strangeness, to say (as is often said by advocates of this point of view) that the facts of the Bible are 'history plus interpretation'? For the distinctive difference between the 'history' of the Gospels and 'ordinary history' will then lie in the 'interpretation'—in the writer's attitude towards the events which each kind of 'history' has in common. The point may be put in another way, and from the standpoint of language. If we say that the facts of the Gospels are 'history plus interpretation', the language of the Gospels would only be 'odd' in the sense that it was a rather complicated version of a simpler language, viz. the 'plainest' history.

In this connection we may perhaps usefully look at some remarks of Professor Dodd. A full discussion would of course have to take carefully into account what he says on the subject in *History and the Gospel*, but for our present purpose it will suffice to refer only to some remarks he has in *The Interpretation of the Fourth Gospel*. I shall suggest that two positions can be distinguished in that book, the first of which, but not the second, would be open to the kind of difficulty we have just raised. The first position tries to make do with the traditional view of 'facts'. It still sponsors the ontology which lay behind the views of Locke and more recent scientific criticism. There is a picture of isolated and objective 'facts' organized by 'minds' which peer at them from a distance. The second position breaks away from this background altogether and is based from the outset on a conviction that the situations to which the Christian appeals are nothing if not odd, that they are ontological peculiars, which is of course a view we can heartily support. Let us look then at the two positions in turn.

In his Appendix titled 'Some considerations upon the historical aspect of the Fourth Gospel', Professor Dodd says the evangelist 'accepts without qualification the general tradition of the ministry, death and resurrection of Jesus, as it was expressed in the apostolic preaching'.[1] Further, 'he has meditated deeply upon the meaning of the Gospel story, taken as a whole'; whereupon he 'turns back upon the details of the story' and seeks to see 'the meaning of the whole' in each 'particular incident'.[2] This is what Dodd would call 'history plus interpretation', and he further says: 'In seeking to interpret the facts he records, the Fourth Evangelist is not necessarily exceeding the limits proper to history.'[3] He is indeed, to use a distinction Dodd has used before, 'the historian, as distinct from the chronicler'.[4]

Dodd argues that there is nothing peculiar about this—even Synoptic Gospels 'have an inseparable element of interpretation in their record'.[5] What, says Dodd, the Fourth Evangelist did, was to relate each episode 'to more rational and more universal ideas'.[6] But this sets in sharp opposition 'episodes' on the one hand and the 'rational ideas'

[1] C. H. Dodd: *The Interpretation of the Fourth Gospel*, C.U.P., 1953, p. 445.
    [2] Ibid.   [3] Ibid.   [4] Ibid.   [5] Loc. cit., p. 446.   [6] Ibid.

with which these episodes are linked on the other, and (not least with nineteenth century idealists in mind) those who search for the distinctiveness of Christianity will prefer to concentrate on the episodes if they mean to make any serious 'appeal' to 'history'. They will wish to attribute some kind of primary importance to the episodical facts. In the Appendix Dodd shows how difficult it is for him to tear himself from this kind of background.

For instance, he says that 'it still remains . . . a part of the task of the student of history to seek to discover (in Ranke's oft-quoted phrase) "wie es eigentlich geschehen ist"—how it actually happened'.[1] From this standpoint Dodd's view is that the Fourth Evangelist is faithful to 'the broad general outline of the ministry, death and resurrection of Jesus Christ which is presupposed in the Synoptic Gospels, reproduced in the apostolic preaching in Acts, and attested up to a point in the Pauline epistles'.[2] It is 'by his fidelity' to this broad general outline that 'the evangelist gives proof of his intention to expound the meaning of facts and not to invent a dramatic plot'.[3] Dodd further argues 'that some probable conclusions might be drawn about the pre-canonical tradition lying behind the *prima facie* historical statements of the Fourth Gospel',[4] and he urges that by a comparison of this tradition with other data drawn for example from the Synoptic Gospels 'we may hope to advance our knowledge of the facts to which they all refer'.[5] Here the implication is that the 'facts' are somehow covered, if not hidden, by tradition and 'interpretation'. Here is a view of facts to which interpretations are somehow added to expound the 'meaning'. But what matters seems to be the 'basic facts', the kind of brute fact, on which subsequently Christian theologians get to work. But then the facts of the Bible are just like 'Queen Anne's death', 'Caesar's crossing the Rubicon',

[1] Loc. cit., p. 447.   [2] Loc. cit., p. 447.   [3] Ibid.
[4] Loc. cit., p. 453.   [5] Ibid.

and they lack significance until some interpretation is put on them. So we have on the one hand an emphasis being laid on the 'facts'—perhaps a hangover from the 'scientific' approach of an earlier day; yet on the other hand an emphasis being laid on 'interpretation' which would bring us perilously near the idealism of the last century. The moral is, I think, not to separate facts and interpretation so sharply; not to sponsor a view of 'facts' which is a legacy from the days of scientific criticism or even earlier days of Locke. The situations to which Christianity appeals are, compared with such 'facts', ontological curiosities; they are, as we have been insisting throughout the book, odd. But this view (as we have said) is only explicitly supported by the second position which can be distinguished in Dodd's book on the Fourth Gospel.

(2) This view may be found usefully summarized on pp. 142-3. There he points out that 'to a writer with the philosophical presuppositions of the evangelist, there is no reason why a narrative should not be at the same time factually true and symbolic of a deeper truth, since things and events of this world derive what reality they possess from the eternal Ideas they embody'.[1] What Dodd does (let us notice) is to distinguish between a narrative being 'factually true' and being symbolic of a 'deeper truth', and he is now emphasizing 'deeper truth'. He has said earlier 'that the events narrated in the Fourth Gospel are intended to be understood as significant events, σημεῖα'.[2] In other words what he is interested in now is not 'brute facts' but 'significant events', which somehow or other are a union of 'things and events of this world' with 'eternal Ideas', a union from which there arises 'deeper truth'. Dodd says rightly that such a view involves a 'fundamental *Weltanschauung*'; that, in other words, the Fourth Evangelist is appealing to the kind of fact about which metaphysicians have talked in their metaphysics, and he continues by saying that the unit of

[1] Loc. cit., pp. 142-3.   [2] Loc. cit., p. 142.

thinking for the Fourth Evangelist is crystallized in the phrase: 'the Word was made flesh'. In other words, the kind of event the Fourth Evangelist is talking about is one whose specimen language is ὁ λόγος σὰρξ ἐγένετο. It is clear, however, that this second view is quite different from the first view, and implies an altogether different ontology.

What we suggest, then, is that Dodd's work on the Fourth Gospel shows that it is not enough to think of the facts of the Bible as 'brute historical facts' to which the Evangelists give distinctive 'interpretations'. Rather are the 'facts' of the Gospels, logically and ontologically, much more complex affairs, having for their typical designation such a logical complexity as ὁ λόγος σὰρξ ἐγένετο. Here is an impropriety indeed. For what more violent mixing of categories could there be than a union of σάρξ—something observable, tangible, and so on—with λόγος—a word which, whatever its specific ancestry and use, had always a reference beyond the perceptual world. In this impropriety, which labels the kind of situation in terms of which the Fourth Evangelist understood and expressed the whole of the Gospel narratives, plainly the significant word is that which links two categories so obviously different, viz. ἐγένετο. Here is a link word, and all we need remark here is that we shall model it only at our peril—doctrinal expositors, please note. To understand it there has to be evoked just that kind of situation which ὁ λόγος σὰρξ ἐγένετο expresses.

What we have done then in this rather lengthy discussion of Dodd has been to show that the claim that the Bible is 'history' is only substantiated if 'history' refers to situations as odd as those which are referred to by that paradigm of the Fourth Gospel: 'the Word became flesh'. What we have now to do is to examine the other, less conservative, development from form-criticism which would claim that a clue to the odd situations which are the subject of the New Testament is given to us in existentialism.

(B) Typical of this new approach of course is Bultmann, and we may usefully refer to a discussion of Bultmann by John Macquarrie.[1] In the course of his book Macquarrie recalls the various attempts which have been made to isolate what he calls the 'objective-historical' elements in the New Testament, and he gives as a specific example the work of the French scholar Guignebert. Macquarrie remarks that Guignebert 'has proved beyond all reasonable doubt' the objective historical reality of the figure of Jesus, though we have to admit (he says) that 'the positive results of his investigation are meagre in the extreme'. However, says Macquarrie, suppose the investigation had been much more positive; suppose Guignebert had not only proved 'the objective historical reality' of Jesus, but had also 'substantially verified' the New Testament record. Would that make much difference for our religious faith or theology? Macquarrie's answer is 'No': 'It would not, and frankly it would be intolerable if it did, for then not only the theologian but the ordinary Christian believer would be at the mercy of the historian.'[2] But why can the believer be so independent of the historian? Because, we are told, what matters, what is 'of primary importance for theology', is the 'existential-historical' element.

But this obviously raises the crucial question as to whether this 'existential-historical' element is then supposed to be altogether independent of what has been called 'the objective historical' element. Incidentally, Macquarrie also considers the dependence of the 'existential-historical' element of what is called the 'mythical' element, but that complication, for our present purpose, need be no more than mentioned.

Faced with such vital questions about the inter-dependency of the elements he distinguishes in the New Testament,

[1] John Macquarrie: *An Existentialist Theology*, S.C.M. Press, 1955.
[2] Loc. cit., p. 170.

Macquarrie admits at one point that all three elements are interwoven, and here, when he asks the question: 'Can theology dispense with any of them?' it is plain that he wishes to say 'No', and this is the general tenor of his argument over pp. 172-9. For instance, he says: 'We would be perfectly willing to agree with Bultmann that Christian theology and Christian preaching must be primarily concerned with the cross as an existential-historical event, for only so can it be a saving event and significant for my existence today. *Yet we must protest at the tendency here to exclude the objective-historical element altogether*' (*italics mine*).[1] Again: 'To preach the cross as a saving event is to propagate an illusion unless the origin of that saving event was an actual happening—namely, God's once-for-all act at Calvary. Bultmann, I believe, recognizes this, but tends to obscure it by excessively subordinating the objective-historical to the existential-historical.'[2] On the other hand, however, he is very soon applauding Bultmann for 'refusing to make theology—and Christian faith—dependent on historical research', suggesting that we can dispense with the 'objective-historical'. The author very honestly admits in a footnote that his discussion 'may seem to require further clarification'. But it is not clear that he gives it to us. He rightly points out in the footnote that there are two possible ways of becoming a Christian. For instance, a man might experience 'a saving event' and infer from that 'an origin for the event in objective world history'. Why he should ever do this, and whether he could in any case 'infer' such an event, are surely difficult questions. However, there is by contrast the man who bases his faith on 'an objective event once occurred'. But we are told, and as much as in the first case, the 'guarantee' lies only in 'the present saving event', even though this may posit 'the once-for-all event as its origin'. I am not now concerned to discuss further the difficulties here. It suffices for my purpose

[1] Loc. cit., pp. 178-9.   [2] Ibid.

that there are difficulties at all and that the 'existential-historical' is only related to the 'objective-historical' problematically. For what I am trying to point out is that on this second, less conservative view, the situations to which the Gospels appeal are odd enough to be called 'existential-historical' where this description implies for either Bultmann or Macquarrie a situation which can neither be identified with, nor made wholly independent of, the 'objective-historical'. An existentialist approach, as we have already recognized, may be helpful in emphasizing the first of these characteristics, but to do that, it compromises, and may even exclude any reasonable account of the other, and there we must part company.

What then is our broad conclusion from these few historical reflections which have brought us to the *philosophical* difficulties with which contemporary biblical theology—whether more or less conservative—presents us? Our conclusions are perhaps two-fold:

1. No attempt to make the language of the Bible conform to a precise straightforward public language—whether that language be scientific or historical—has ever succeeded.

2. More positively, the Bible is about situations as odd as those which we have had in mind throughout this book; the kind of situation to which existentialists refer when they speak of something being 'authentic' or 'existential-historical'. The 'facts' of the Gospels in particular are never facts for which science is appropriate currency, or history is appropriate currency. The paradigm is ὁ λόγος σὰρξ ἐγένετο.

In all, we must recognize that the language of the Bible, and of the Gospels in particular, must be odd enough to be appropriate to the odd situations which are their subject. If then we are to resolve the philosophical difficulties which biblical criticism presents to us, we will have to gain more insight into the peculiar *logical* structure the evangelists gave to their language when they wrote the Gospels to tell of the 'wonderful works of God'. Already we can understand afresh the traditional description of the Bible as 'the Word of God'. From the outset we must recognize the logical peculiarity of this phrase. Sometimes when it is said that 'the Bible is "the Word of God" ' this is taken as equivalent to 'the Bible is "the Words of God" '. Hence arises the picture of God as some high executive, with the Bible as a tape recorder. But this picture only arises if we make the erroneous and straight-forward translation. Otherwise, let us take 'word' as a model, just as we would take 'verbal' as a model if we wished to speak alternatively of the 'verbal inspiration' of the Bible. To talk of the Bible as 'the Word of God' or as 'verbally inspired' is then to claim that if we take the words of the Bible and follow out the verbal pattern they form, the light will dawn, the ice will break, and so on. There will be once again a situation of 'challenge' and 'response'—the sort of situation which is called 'holy'. So we speak indeed of 'hearing' and 'receiving' God's holy Word. If this kind of characteristic situation is not evoked, we shall not know what it means to claim that the Bible is 'the Word of God', or that the Bible is 'verbally inspired'.

Further, we can now see how more needs to be said, and can be said, about the New Testament than the phrase 'Word of God' by itself necessarily implies. The New Testament is that *and more*. For the illumination of the New Testament goes beyond that of the Old, the 'situations' which the New Testament is about go beyond those of the Old, precisely as 'the fleshly Word of God' goes beyond the un-qualified 'Word of God'. We may say if we wish that the whole Bible is 'the Word of God', meaning that the kind of situations to which its words refer are situations of the kind we have mentioned in relation to which the word 'God' is posited. But more has to be said—there has to be some further qualifier—to make plain the distinctive character of the New Testament.

Having now justified in a general way our original claim that the language of the Bible is not logically plain and straightforward, let us illustrate this claim by means of some particular examples which approach the Bible with an eye to the logical structure of its narratives.

A. *Naming God*

It is a well-known fact of Old Testament theology that the Hebrews were nervous about naming God and that in particular the sacred *Tetragrammaton* was never pronounced. I think that what we have said enables us to see the philosophical significance of these habits, and altogether there are three points we might usefully make.

(a) To be told anyone's name is, as we saw in the first chapter, a possible occasion for the 'ice to break'. We are going along a country lane one spring afternoon and see a man sitting in the ditch, mopping the sweat off his brow, and think of him as a loyal county council employee. We ask him the way to some neighbouring hamlet and he replies in an astonishingly cultured voice that he does not know the neighbourhood at all; then we see (by his side) a Treasury bag and even (we may suppose) that unique red dispatch box and the truth dawns . . . here is old Jimmy Windbag working out his Budget proposals. We see the man as he 'really is'. The situation, which before had been so tractable in ordinary language of villages, ditches and workmen, becomes a disclosure; becomes characteristically different, takes on depth. Again, to repeat an example, we all know how the ice breaks at a conference when we see names on lapels. It is not just a matter of extra information, but there is a gain in what is sometimes called 'human warmth'.

The word which names a person belongs then to a disclosure situation, to a situation which has a religious significance, so that it is not surprising that naming has always had the religious associations it has had. For someone to tell us his name may be, and in a full sense always is to be, bound up with him in a characteristic religious situation. Those who tell us their names have granted us a discernment to which there has been a characteristically personal response. We have 'accepted' just that name for that 'person'.

(b) Secondly, let it be noticed that naming only has a religious significance when the name is disclosed to us and not when we ourselves choose the name. We may, for instance, name in the sense of label without there being any religious activity whatever. So Russell with his 'ostensive definitions'. But for us, to name in what we may call the 'full' sense, would mean that it was in our power to will and create a religious situation, and thus to guarantee God, to compel a religious disclosure, and this the religious man would never allow possible. If *we* name, there is no disclosure. There are, however, two apparent exceptions to that generalization. What, it may be said, of the explorer who names a territory into which none has ventured before? Certainly we cannot claim here in any obvious sense that the name is 'disclosed'. Yet is not this act of naming characteristically religious? What do we make of this apparent exception? I suggest that what happens here is that we have *already* a characteristically religious situation, evoked when the explorer steps into hitherto unknown and untrodden land. For here is mystery and awe in large measure. It is in such a setting that he gives a name to the new country, but what belongs intrinsically to the disclosure is not the explorer's label but God's presence, and the most the explorer can do to represent the situation in all its fullness is to associate his own label with God's name, the name he first knew in a disclosure of this kind. Hence the explorer 'dedicates' a land, i.e. he labels it, but more 'In the name of God'. In ways such as these, the naming of the land is incorporated with a specifically worshipful situation; even though it is the explorer who is naming, there is a disclosure, but it has occurred previously and independently and what the explorer does is to make his labelling one with the disclosure situation which anticipated it.

Or again, another exception—that of baptism, where apparently *we* name a child. Indeed, in the Anglican rite, the request is made explicitly: 'Name this child'. But this is no more than labelling, and indeed the word uttered is not the child's Christian name until it has been suitably qualified, associated (as in the explorer case) with a worshipful situation, with the name of the Father and of the Son and of the Holy Ghost, whereupon we speak of the child as 'a child of God'. Once again a label becomes a name when it has been brought into a worshipful situation by virtue of which there is already a 'disclosure'. So, despite these apparent exceptions of the explorer and of baptism, we can still make the broad generalization that it is only when a 'name' is disclosed to us by the person himself, that a situation is characteristically religious. If *we* name, there is no disclosure.

(c) It is with this background that we can consider the well-known passages in Ex., Chapters 3 and 6.

(1) It is interesting to notice that in Ex. 3, when God apparently discloses his name unambiguously, the logical structure of the phrase given as God's name is suited to what we have called a characteristically religious situation. For as we saw in our first chapter, the significant tautology 'I'm I' discloses a final option, the kind of option which characterizes religious loyalty. But this is plainly a phrase whose logical structure portrays primarily the character of religious commitment; it is not at all a personal proper name.

In other words, when in Ex. 3 a phrase is given as the name of God, it is not so much a name of God as a phrase which could be posited by the religious man to do justice to the commitment his religion carries with it. To this extent the variant translations given by the revisers are not only superfluous but misleading and conceal the true logical point of the tautology. 'I am because I am', which looks as though God is a philosopher confessing himself as 'self-caused'; or 'I am who am'—taken to represent 'He who is' or 'necessary Being'; or 'I will be that I will be' considered as a promise of God's faithfulness—all these variants, however possible in the Hebrew, and however instructive as commentaries on it, are all of them endeavours to make what is rightly tautological, not so; they are all endeavours to get some kind of straightforward assertion from a phrase whose logical structure has a very different tale to tell.

So far then, when it has been claimed that God has disclosed his name, what we have, in fact, is a characteristically religious situation with language appropriate to such a situation. Anything like a 'name' escapes us. What is given in Ex. 3 as the name of God, is not a 'name', as we would expect a name, but a phrase which is the best phrase men can use to talk of that full commitment in which his loyalty to God is expressed.

(2) God's name itself ever remains mysterious, and that of logical necessity. Why? I think the following considerations may be given by way of answer. We have seen that when a name is first vouchsafed to us there is the kind of disclosure which we have called characteristically religious. But it is unfortunately the case, as we should all recognize, that such a 'name' can only too easily become a 'label'. What was once a disclosure can very soon become drained of its religious significance. Human warmth can freeze and friendship become formal. If then we could say that on some occasion God had fully vouchsafed his name, might it not soon lead to a theological formalism of the most idolatrous brand?

So, if God is always to be known in a disclosure situation, and recognizing that, if we were vouchsafed with God's name, our vision might soon become atrophied—loving the name more than him who had disclosed it—we can only meet this difficulty by supposing that the name of God will never at any time be *completely* vouchsafed to us. Expressing the point somewhat differently, and if we wish to speak in terms of God's 'name', we might say that a characteristically religious situation resembles one where a person is always *about* to disclose to us his name, but never fully does so.

Hence, when God's name is disclosed to us in Ex. 6; disclosed to Moses as it was not to Isaac, Abraham or Jacob, it is now inevitably approximate, suitably mysterious. Here is the logical merit of the sacred *Tetragrammaton*. It is as though in some panel game we had the consonants JHVH and no matter how far the game went on we never succeeded in choosing the appropriate vowels. Only God could know the answer. Only God could know his own name. Otherwise, the permanent irreducibility of a religious situation might be lost. The inevitable elusiveness of the divine name is the logical safeguard against universal idolatry. So it is that the sacred *Tetragrammaton* is the furthest we could ever go in having a 'name' for God, and it is *quite essential* that such a name should be unpronounceable in its fulness. Meanwhile, let us notice that JHVH is a real advance on (say) *El Shaddai*. *El Shaddai*, as God appeared to Abraham, Isaac and Jacob, is, philosophically speaking, no more than a qualified model and would witness to no more than a *general* religious situation. But JHVH witnesses to a religious situation for whose understanding we need *personal* categories, for it is isomorphous, though not identical, with those situations when a person discloses to us his name.

B. *Prophecy*

For our second example let us look at the concept of prophecy. What is prophecy? I suggest that in the widest sense the word relates once again to a 'disclosure', to what we have called a characteristically theological situation. If we look for a typical example we need not go to the ninth or seventh centuries B.C. The example comes just as well from the earlier story of David and Nathan in II Sam. 12.1-7. There are the two men in one city; 'the one rich and the other poor'. The rich man has many flocks and herds; the poor man has nothing save one little ewe lamb. Along come guests; the rich man hesitates to kill his own cattle; takes the poor man's lamb and prepares it for his great dinner. Here is an 'objective' story. Faced with this situation David judges that the man who did this is 'worthy to die' and 'shall restore the lamb four-fold'. So far the story is one which might have been told in a Law Court, and David has given an objective judgment on it. So far there is no 'prophecy' at all. So far the prophetic mission of Nathan is not obvious. The characteristic touch only comes in verse 7: 'Thou art the man.' The penny drops; there is indeed a disclosure. David recognizes that the story is about none other than— *himself*. It is significant that at this point, when there has been this disclosure, the language traditionally used for prophetic insight becomes at once appropriate currency; 'Thus saith the Lord'.

In this way then, prophetic language is disclosure language. But there is more to say about it than that. Let us look a little further at II Sam. 12. Nathan reviews the kindness of God towards David; condemns David because he has despised God; and then 'prophesies' to David that God will consequently 'raise up evil against thee out of thine own house'. Now what is 'prophesied' in this way becomes, does it not, an expression of what is disclosed? It formulates the disclosure. 'What God will purpose' is the currency used to declare what God is, as disclosed. In this way, purposive prediction language becomes, in prophecy, the currency for speaking about disclosure. Incidentally, we are hinting at the possibility of such a logical device when we speak of an 'impressive man' being 'full of promise'.

Sometimes of course, perhaps in most prophecies, there is no separate story like that of the little ewe lamb by means of which the disclosure is effected. In such cases the disclosure is alternatively effected by portraying some situation which *contrasts violently* with present circumstances, and the technique for portraying such a contrast is a prediction story which, as before, then serves as currency for the disclosure. A contrasting story is told, whose point is to evoke, when set against a given environment, a characteristically religious situation. When this disclosure occurs, the story then also provides us with its purposive prediction language as currency for the disclosure itself.

For example, in a land where nature is nothing if not 'red in tooth and claw'; where none but the strongest of men could measure up to the challenge of their environment, a disclosure was effected by telling a contrasting story in purposive prediction language which looked to a time when 'the wolf shall dwell with the lamb and the leopard shall lie down with the kid, and the calf and the young lion and the fatling together, and a little child shall lead them' (Isa. 11.6). Or again, when Israel was threatened on all sides, a disclosure was effected, and expressed by a contrasting story in purposive prediction language, by speaking of a time when 'the labour of Egypt and the merchandise of Ethiopia, and the Sabeans, men of stature, shall come over unto thee and . . . be thine; . . . in chains they shall come over: and they shall fall down unto thee' (Isa. 45.14).

Here then is prophecy as a 'disclosure'; and we have also tried to show the twofold logical significance of the purposive predictive language which the prophets used *viz.*: to evoke the disclosure and to be currency for that which is disclosed. This naturally leads us to ask what can be meant by *fulfilment* of prophecy, but before discussing that topic there are one or two further points to make on prophecy in general.

For instance, it accords with what we have been saying,

that the prophets criticize formal worship. They see that situations lose their religious distinctiveness, that they lose 'depth', when they become impersonal. It is then that men bow down their heads merely 'as a rush'[1]—and what could be more objective, formal and impersonal than that? At the same time there comes a loss of moral insight. With that reflection we can go on to see the logical merit of the Eighth and Seventh century prophets. They saw, like Butler, that a characteristically religious situation was homogeneous with situations of morality; and they claimed that its discernment logically entailed the discernment of an obligation, the discernment of a duty which called for a moral response, as an appropriate commitment.

In this way we see how for the Eight and Seventh century prophets ethical words like 'mercy' and 'justice' become currency in which to talk of the challenge of God. On the other hand they are not by themselves adequate currency for theology, and here is the well-known contention that the Eighth and Seventh century prophets were not moralists; while the prophetic message uses ethical words it inevitably goes beyond the language of morals. For instance, in Hosea, a personal story of a moral kind only speaks of God when it is suitably qualified. The story is introduced by the sentence 'When the Lord spake at the first with Hosea, the Lord said unto Hosea, Go take unto thee a wife of whoredom and children of whoredom . . .'.[2] In this way the whole story is defined by and enclosed within the operator 'Thus said the Lord' ='The Lord said unto Hosea'. Here is an operator, or as it were a bracket, which gives the moral story theological status. Further, the various names of the children ensure that the story shall be set in relation to the pattern of events in Israel, in the hope that when the story is placed against this wider background there may be evoked that depth, that characteristic situation, that challenge, which

[1] Isa. 58.5.   [2] Hos. 1.2.

Hosea is under divine compulsion to make evident to those around him. For another method of effecting a disclosure—besides the method of contrasts—is to see one story as surprisingly interconnected with another. In these ways, the story is a moral tale *and more*. For it is a moral story which makes a religious point when it is associated with a wider historical background, whereupon the whole can be taken under the general directive: 'Thus saith the Lord'.

What now of prophecy fulfilment? What do we mean by saying that prophecies are 'fulfilled'? There are broadly two answers, and while the first is the one which most easily comes to mind, I shall also argue that it is the least important.

(a) A prophecy might be said to be 'fulfilled' if its purposive prediction language was verified in fact; if the prophecies in this sense 'came off'. This would be the sense in which a weather forecast is verified (or not) by the way the weather develops; or a scientific prediction about the properties of a hitherto unknown element is subsequently verified (or not) when the element is isolated. Here would be prophecy-fulfilment in the strict scientific sense so dear to the eighteenth century. But if it is no more than what we have suggested, prophecy-fulfilment could hardly have a very important and distinctive religious point. Indeed, its religious point could be equally well made by *any* prediction which came off: it might, in other words, enable us to talk about the reliability of God, his providential control and so on. But further it would not take us. At best, it would enable us to talk of God in terms of some large-scale purpose.

At the same time let us not do an injustice to the eighteenth century, as we certainly do if we say that for them prophecy was no more than prediction. For we have to remember how 'wonderful' scientific prediction seemed to that century. For many eighteenth-century people it was scientific prediction that when verified made situations come alive. They did their mathematics; predicted an eclipse; went up a

mountain; set their watches; zero hour approached, and . . .
it happened! Here was a wonderful disclosure; here was
worship; and for the eighteenth century what then could be
better currency than scientific prediction for talking about
such situations?

What I want to suggest, therefore, is that the eighteenth
century may have had an idea of prophecy fulfilment which
was far more religious than talk about predictions coming
off might suggest. What they lacked indeed was a logically
satisfactory way of talking about it. Certainly, to speak of
prophecies fulfilled and to talk of predictions scientifically
verified, is to play two different logical games.

(b) So much then for the first, and to some degree unsatisfactory, answer to the question: What is meant when we say that
prophecies are 'fulfilled'? What now of the second answer?
Let us first give it in general terms and then pass to two
examples, the second of which raises a new point altogether.

I suggest that prophetic language is 'fulfilled' in this
second sense if it is the case that, not merely does it look back
to a retrospective disclosure, but in its turn, when brought
alongside some situation or other, it generates a second
disclosure. Let us now illustrate this generalization, and take
first of all a simple case, the disclosure language of Isa. 7.
14-16:

'Therefore the Lord himself shall give you a sign; behold,
a virgin shall conceive, and bear a son, and shall call his
name Immanuel. Butter and honey shall he eat, when he
knoweth to refuse the evil, and choose the good. For before
the child shall know to refuse evil, and choose the good, the
land whose two kings thou abhorrest shall be forsaken.'

Here in Judah was an apparently hopeless situation. 'Rezin
the King of Syria, and Pekah the son of Remaliah, King of
Israel, went up to Jerusalem to war against it'. These 'two
tails of smoking firebrands' moved the hearts of the people
(Isa. 7.1-6). So a story is told as in the case of David and

Nathan. Already within this apparently hopeless situation—
with Jerusalem besieged by two kings—it is 'prophesied'
that a maiden is with child, and the son to be born shall
bear the name 'Emmanuel', i.e. 'God is with us'. The intention is that the whole depressing situation will be transformed once this story of the maiden is brought alongside,
and that such a transformation will come about as soon as
we see how this element within the total situation epitomizes
the whole. Thereupon (it is hoped) the penny will drop,
and the light break. What seems so clearly to human eyes a
hopeless situation; a situation productive only of travail,
has nevertheless hope and promise about it. Before the child
can eat 'butter and honey' . . . 'the land whose two kings
thou abhorrest shall be forsaken'. Here once again is purposive prediction language which, brought alongside certain
facts, effects a disclosure. Here is language which, together
with a certain pattern of facts, gives rise to a disclosure.

Now recalling our first sense of 'fulfilment' it may be said
that this prophecy was *in that sense* 'fulfilled' if and when the
child was born; if and when the land of the two kings was
forsaken before in fact the child ate butter and honey. But
even if that were so, it would add nothing of great religious
significance to the disclosure that had already occurred.
There would be a sort of scientific fulfilment, but (as we
have seen) that would have no *special* religious merit. Indeed,
had there been *no* fulfilment in such a scientific sense, the
religious man of the day would not have been particularly
troubled; he was quite used to events turning out rather
differently from what he expected, and though there might
be a long story to tell in detail, he would be quite sure that
in the end he would be able to include the unexpected
variation within his God-loyalty.

But that first sense of 'fulfilment' apart, there is another,
and for us a more important, sense in which this prophecy is
'fulfilled', and that would be the sense which is used in Matt.

1.22, when the prophecy is said to be 'fulfilled' in Jesus. What happens now is that this language is brought alongside other facts which are plainly quite different from the original facts in relation to which there was the *original* disclosure, and the claim is that there is now a *further* disclosure. Or, putting the matter in another way: here was the birth of Jesus, itself the occasion of a 'disclosure', and those who were concerned to proclaim to others this situation which, for them, was so significant, looked for language which, when brought alongside this 'wonderful' situation, might evoke a characteristic disclosure for their readers, and so prove to be currency for what they contrived to express. Such language they found in Isa. 7.14. Let me not at all conceal the fact that in a curious way there is a gap between the prophetic language and the situation about which it is used when there is a 'fulfilment'. I admit that at the moment I cannot see that any logical treatment can be given to this gap, and perhaps that is because it cannot have any *logical* treatment at all. At any rate we can recall that there was a similar gap when the prophecy was originally formulated; and *some* sort of 'gap' seems to be needful if there is to be any disclosure at all. However, I hope I have made the second type of prophecy-fulfilment clear. 'Fulfilment' in this second sense occurs when the language used of *one* disclosure is used in relation to *other* facts for a *second* disclosure. Fulfilment of prophecy relates to what might thus be called, a disclosure beyond a disclosure; a second order disclosure.

Let us now consider, as a second example, a rather more complex case which leads to some reflections about Apocalyptic. Consider a case where it was expected that the purposive prediction language would be fulfilled in a scientific sense, and where to date it had not been. Here would be language in search of a situation of one or both of two kinds. There might arise on the one hand a situation which accurately verified the language in a scientific sense; alternatively there might arise a situation from whose juxtaposition with the language there came a second and further disclosure. When the language is regarded from the first point of view, it has the logic of an apocalyptic narrative; when the language is regarded from the second point of view its logic is that which belongs to one Christian use of the Old Testament. The important conclusion is that here we have two different kinds of logical behaviour and it is hardly likely that we shall confuse them with impunity. The greatest logical caution, therefore, will be needed before we read off the Christian message in terms of Apocalyptic; or before we try to express the 'apocalyptic' element in the Christian message. That reflection leads to wider questions we cannot at the moment discuss,[1] and all I am concerned to do now is to insist on the logical distinction I have just drawn—between language used apocalyptically, and language used to talk of Christian 'fulfilment'. Without doubt, and of necessity, it was in the first sense—of 'apocalyptic'—that the Old Testament thought of prophecy-*fulfilment*: the prophetic language had already had its religious significance with the retrospective disclosure, and nothing remained to look for, but its strict verification. Consider, for example, the following verses:

'Thus saith the Lord, the labour of Egypt, and the merchandise of Ethiopia, and the Sabeans, men of stature, shall come over unto thee, and they shall be thine; they shall go after thee; in chains they shall come over; and they shall fall down unto thee, they shall make supplication unto thee saying, Surely God is in thee; and there is none else, there is no God.'[2] Or:

'For behold, the Lord will come with fire, and his chariots shall be like the whirlwind; to render his anger with fury, and his rebuke with flames of fire. For by fire will the Lord

[1] E.g. How far does the Christian regard the 'Second Coming' as something to be scientifically verified; how far as a future and further 'fulfilment'?

[2] Isa. 45.14.

plead, and by his sword, with all flesh: and the slain of the Lord shall be many. . . . And they shall bring all your brethren out of all the nations for an offering unto the Lord, upon horses, and in chariots, and in litters, and upon mules, and upon swift beasts, to my holy mountain Jerusalem, saith the Lord, as the children of Israel bring their offering in a clean vessel into the house of the Lord. . . . And they shall go forth, and look upon the carcases of the men that have transgressed against me; for their worm shall not die, neither shall their fire be quenched; and they shall be an abhorring unto all flesh.'[1]

These may be taken as describing actual hopes which would be 'fulfilled' when the facts accorded with their pre-dictions, when men appeared in chains, the brethren arrived on swift beasts, and so on. The language of Apocalyp-tic is in this way the language of verifiable predictions; but the same language, as 'prophecy', will *already* have had its other (and we might think major) 'disclosure' function when it has been used to evoke a characteristically religious situa-tion in virtue of the contrast between its theme on the one hand and what its hearers saw around them on the other.

Further, the same language only becomes currency for New Testament 'fulfilment' when its relation to New Testament events is such that a *second* disclosure is evoked. It is then imperative, as we saw before, that New Testament events must *not* be exactly covered or 'predicted' by the language of Apocalyptic, or else there would be no more in the New Testament than had already been disclosed in the Old. We are back again at the gap we have already noticed between the Old Testament language and the New Testament facts; a gap which is essential if the distinctive-ness of the Christian message is to be preserved, but a gap for which I readily confess I have found no logical bridge. But what I hope I have at least done is to show how we can

[1] Isa. 66.15, 16, 20, 24.

(and must) distinguish between prophecy, verifiable predictions, apocalyptic, and prophecy-fulfilment, while relating each in its own way to what we have called characteristically-religious situations.

C. *The New Testament narratives: Virgin Birth, Crucifixion, Resurrection, Ascension*

We now pass to some examples from the New Testament itself. We have already urged that the Gospels are not plain 'history'—they can be said to refer to 'historical' situations only if this is history with a difference. It is this difference which, as we saw, Dodd tried to express by speaking of history *plus* interpretation, or fact *plus* occurrence; which (much better) he implied in his notion of a 'deeper truth' expressed by such an impropriety as John 1.14; something which Bultmann elucidated from another direction altogether in terms of an 'existential' approach. Together, both Dodd and Bultmann emphasize the logical oddness of the gospel language, and the empirical peculiarity of those situations to which this language refers.

What I would like to show now, by means of examples, is that the language used in the New Testament is appropriate currency for the kind of odd situation the Gospels are about. Perhaps it is not too rash to suggest that these examples hint at the possibility of a further stage in our understanding of the New Testament. As Source-criticism (with its *scientific* approach) yielded to Form-criticism (with its *literary* approach) may not the time be opportune for Form-criticism to give place to a *logical* approach? In passing, I would suggest incidentally that the difficulties of typology—however much we may welcome the inspiration which expresses itself through the fertile literary imaginations of its expositors—arise for the most part from its lack of logical restraint, from a lack of any principles of logical control. It is just such a control which a logical approach to the Gospels, of the kind

I have in mind, might be expected *inter alia* to provide. Such an approach might be called not so much logical 'criticism' as logical analysis, if this phrase could best describe the search for appropriate logical structures in the Gospel narratives, which the following illustrations, I hope, will do something to exemplify, even if they do not go very far. Our first two examples, the one from St Mark's Gospel, the other from the Fourth Gospel, support incidentally the view that the Synoptics and the Fourth Gospel are not as far apart as once they were thought to be.

Let it be supposed, for the sake of argument, that the language of St Mark's Gospel is of all the Gospels most straightforward, and least characterized by impropriety. Many would contend with that assertion, so let me emphasize that I am only taking it for the sake of an example. Equally, for the sake of example, let us suppose that Dr R. H. Lightfoot was right in his main point about the ending of St Mark's Gospel. Then it would be here especially that impropriety and disclosure came to their own: ἐφοβοῦντο γάρ.[1] Not only would there be the point that this was not 'fear' in the ordinary sense of 'fear', but fear in the sense of 'religious awe'. The further point would now be made that in order to be appropriate currency for the disclosure situation, which on this view was the end-climax of the Gospel, some kind of impropriety was *essential*. What could be better than ἐφοβοῦντο γάρ . . . leaving us there, in the hope that the ice would break, the light dawn, the penny drop . . . that we should be caught up in the 'awe' of the first believers, 'see' and 'respond'?

Our second example comes from the Fourth Gospel with its many conversations at cross purposes, and all its play on words. Right from the start the language of the Gospel is much more improper; it emphasizes much more than St Mark's Gospel the oddness of those situations which it is trying to

[1] Mark 16.8.

proclaim. Hence its traditional description as 'spiritual', even when that did no justice to its strong empirical interests which have at all costs to be equally emphasized, and indeed were meant to be emphasized by their author.

Consider, as a particular example, the story of the woman of Samaria in John 4. Jesus, weary and thirsty, needs water to drink and makes his request to the woman: 'Give me to drink'.[1] For a Samaritan woman the situation is admittedly puzzling and odd. But it is only conventionally puzzling—there is so far no *revealing* impropriety. 'How is it that thou, being a Jew, asks drink of me which am a Samaritan woman? (For Jews have no dealings with Samaritans).'[2] Here are accepted distinctions—men and women, Jews and Samaritans—conventional distinctions which the request of Jesus suffices to challenge, and in this way provokes an initial puzzlement, but no more.

Now at this point Jesus offers 'living water'.[3] To the woman this was even more puzzling, but again it was not because of any *revealing* impropriety. It was just that here was a thirsty man not only offering water, but going one better than Jacob's well, and offering living water, i.e. running water. 'Living water' (let it be noticed) is seen as no logical impropriety, as nothing extraordinary. The Samaritan woman insists on translating the phrase into something quite straightforward, i.e. running water, whereupon there are more puzzles of the unrevealing sort: 'But you have nothing to draw with'; 'Must not the running water be deeper than this well?', and so on.

At this point Jesus shoots into the situation another language altogether, which may or may not have been suggested by his insight into the character of the woman and her general demeanour with him; 'Go call thy husband'.[4] Here is a shock; the light begins to break; the situation begins to come alive. There has been a disclosure; so much so, that

[1] John 4.7.　　[2] John 4.9.　　[3] John 4.10.　　[4] John 4.16.

the word 'prophet' can be used. 'Sir, I perceive that thou art a prophet.'[1] There is not yet, however, a 'full' disclosure —we are rather at the level of the Old Testament prophecies which have not been Christianly fulfilled. But there has been sufficient of a disclosure to justify a move to theological language as being more appropriate currency for the situation: 'Tradition says so and so; you prophets say so and so, and then there is this Messiah, this Christ, who will come and declare all things.'[2] She knows her theology well enough; but even a theological frame does not guarantee the picture. Not even theological language, odd as it is, *necessarily* guarantees the fullest vision. The last move has to be from Jesus himself. 'I that speak unto thee am he.'[3] Perhaps the Greek better expresses the oddness of the challenge: 'Eγώ εἰμι, ὁ λαλῶν σοι. 'I . . . I am . . . speaking . . . to you. . . .' Here is not only the 'I am I' to which we have referred already; but here is 'I' embracing the description 'Messiah' *and more*; there is so much more in *this* challenge than ever descriptive theology could cover. Here is a disclosure which has only been evoked when 'thirsty Jew' becomes 'strange water purveyor', becomes 'prophet', becomes 'Messiah', becomes 'I . . . speaking . . . to you'. Only then does the light break, eyes are opened, and there is a *Christian* disclosure. Once again we see that a Gospel-situation is one for whose expression language must be used with logical impropriety. How much better it would have been if the English translators had been able to leave the phrase as close as possible to the Greek original rather than to give it the appearance of a straightforward cut and dried assertion, whereupon the mystery disappears. From 'I that speaketh to thee am he', we can only too easily (and wrongly) conclude that Jesus accepted without qualification the label 'Messiah': that the definite description was an exact fit. But as we have stressed *ad nauseam*, the Gospels tell of situations which are publicly

[1] John 4.19.   [2] Cp. John 4.25.   [3] John 4.26.

describable *and more*, 'mysterious' situations whose language cannot be straightforward. This was the point that stories about 'fact' and 'interpretation' tried to make, but they did it in a logic which made their task self-defeating. It is *logically* impossible for Jesus to be 'the Messiah'.

For the next example, let us look at three major events of the Christian dispensation and see what useful reflections we can make on them from a logical standpoint—the Crucifixion, the Resurrection, the Ascension and a place will be found in the discussion for some thoughts on the Virgin Birth. On the face of it these events seem to fall in a graded series: the Crucifixion seems very straightforward and readily understood by all; the Resurrection, however, somewhat puzzling; the Ascension distinctively so. Indeed, preachers have been known who were somewhat thankful that Ascension Day falls on a Thursday. But our conclusion will be that such grading is mistaken; and such thankfulness misplaced.

First is the Crucifixion all that straightforward? It is true that Christians believe that Jesus of Nazareth was 'crucified . . . under Pontius Pilate, suffered and was buried' as the Nicene Creed has it. Or alternatively in the phrases of the Apostles' Creed, the Christian belief is that Jesus 'suffered under Pontius Pilate, was crucified, dead and buried'. Certainly such phrases, as they stand, are very straightforward; but *as they stand* they are not specifically Christian. Countless people could utter with conviction the phrases I have mentioned, but if they believed only these, they need not at all be Christian. Everybody who did the equivalent of buying an evening newspaper or listening to the news, in something like A.D. 33, ought to have believed all these phrases; but plainly not everybody could be called Christian. So the point formulates itself that the phrases we have just mentioned are important and are apt currency for Christian commitment *only because* they are related to everything else which surrounds them in the whole setting of the Creeds. Here indeed is the logical point of such a phrase as the Nicene Creed introduces 'for us'. To understand that grammatically slight yet logically essential phrase we need to develop the whole of Christian doctrine. Here is the phrase which expresses and emphasizes the fact that the Crucifixion, for the Christian, was an occasion suitably odd. Indeed, the word 'crucifixion' by itself conceals this point. It does not differentiate sufficiently between the three crucifixions that tradition tells us occurred on the same day and in the same place. Not for nothing have Christians usually spoken, not of the Crucifixion, but of the Cross.

Having now pointed out that, for the Christian, the Crucifixion is no straightforward 'fact', let us now turn to consider the Resurrection. Since the Crucifixion has proved odder than we expected, it has, by implication, already prepared us for our approach to the Resurrection.

Suppose we begin by asking the question which many others have asked: 'Did the Resurrection occur?' It sounds a very simple, straightforward, question, like: 'Did Queen Anne's death occur?' But a moment's reflection makes it plain that, and not for the first time, grammatical similarities may be deceptive. If the word 'Resurrection' refers to such 'data' as an 'empty tomb', visions, etc. all these might not only have happened but be believed, without in any sense there being a Christian belief in the Resurrection; without there being Christian commitment. It might, for instance, always be said that there was an earthquake; that parallels could be drawn from abnormal psychology, and so on. So, 'Did the Resurrection occur?' has *not* the same logic as 'Did the empty tomb occur?' if for no other reason than that the second can be asserted while the first is denied, and the second might even be, and by some has been, denied while the first has been asserted. What then can we say about it?

My suggestion is, that 'Did the Resurrection occur?', while

being no logical kinsman of 'Did Queen Anne's death occur?', is logically much more similar to our asking in regard of a certain situation 'Is that a case of duty? Is that a case of genuine personal devotion?' We can recall from Chapter I the example of the man saving the drowning child. Clearly, evidence is relevant to our answering the question 'Is that a case of duty?' We see the man's momentary hesitation, his dive in, his gripping the child, his exhausted condition as they both come to the bank . . . all this leads us to congratulate him on his sense of duty. But the sceptic on the bank could say 'Not necessarily so'; and he could, in all kinds of whispers, formulate alternatives. The 'hero' might have saved the child because he hoped to ingratiate himself with the parents; he might have saved the child to get a reward; he might have saved the child for no more than self-display, and the momentary hesitation beforehand was all part of the deception; who knows? His diving in may have been the work of some instinct or complex, and the rest; even more, he might have jumped in because he was frightened lest he be accused of neglect or callousness. He might have yielded to no more than supposed public opinion. And if the current proved too strong and he and the child were drowned, the sceptic might still whisper that it was only a few days before that the man had said he had had enough of life and might not this have been suicide? And so on.

In other words, here again we have a question, for the answering of which evidence is relevant; but the evidence might all be believed without the question itself being answered in the affirmative. In both the case of the drowning child and the case of the Resurrection, 'evidence' has a strange empirical relevance. It must certainly be examined, and as we have said, is undoubtedly relevant. But in each case the puzzle arises that no amount of 'evidence' alone guarantees that in relation to which it is considered, namely, the 'Resurrection' on the one hand, or 'duty' on the other.

May not this be because no amount of 'evidence' alone can guarantee what exceeds all the evidence taken together: something which is spatio-temporal and more? 'Resurrection', like 'duty' and 'love', all specify occasions—as our examples in Chapter I would remind us—for which a whole host of empirical criteria are relevant, but these criteria are organized by, and are never exhaustive evidence for the loyalties they name. None of the criteria in itself guarantees that situation—discernment-response—which exceeds them all.

Once again we see how the Christian faith centres on an odd situation, and it is precisely such an odd situation which the language of the Gospels somehow or other must, and does, evoke. As we have noticed, and supposing Lightfoot is right, the impropriety of Mark 16.8 would bespeak such a situation. Again, is it not significant that the 'Risen Christ' was known in the garden, when the situation came alive, by the use of the personal intimate name 'Mary'?[1] Here was a situation for which the general name, the trade name, the impersonal term 'the gardener'[2] had not been sufficient. Again, at the moment when the 'Risen Christ' is known in the village house in Emmaus, he ceases to be 'seen' in a perceptual sense: '. . . their eyes were opened and they knew him; and he vanished out of their sight'.[3] What is distinctive and important about the risen Christ is something other than 'what's seen'. The hearts of the two travellers may have 'burned' within them 'in the way',[4] but the penny had not fully dropped, the light had not then dawned. As the Greek text suggests, their hearts at this point had only been 'ignited'.[5] When the flame leapt up, and the full disclosure came, there was a situation whose significance lay in its *oddness*; a situation in which the risen Christ was 'known', though he had 'vanished out of their sight'.[6] The Resurrection is nothing if not odd.

---

[1] John 20.16. [2] John 20.15. [3] Luke 24.31.
[4] Luke 24.32. [5] καιομένη. [6] Luke 24.31.

Let me make two further points:

(a) First, what about 'dating' the Resurrection? Plainly, in so far as the Resurrection concerns observational events which have a place in time, it can be dated as much as the Crucifixion can be dated. We can, for instance, date the Empty Tomb. But what I have been saying implies that, *taken as a whole*, that to which the word 'Resurrection' applies cannot be dated, simply because the language of dating is just not appropriate for a situation which is not only spatio-temporal, *but more*. We cannot *date* the *Resurrection*: any more than we can walk out with Pythagoras' Theorem or find the square root of love. Again, the Resurrection cannot in strict truth be dated any more than 'duty' can be wholly exhausted by a story of spatio-temporal consequences. So, when we confess that 'the third day He rose again from the dead', the confession has sufficient logical impropriety to be appropriate currency for what the Christian believes about the Resurrection. It is logically very distant from a grammatical parallel such as 'The third day he rose again from his bed'.

(b) The second point: From another angle, what all this amounts to saying is that—*strictly and carefully* speaking—no one can be doubtful about the 'Resurrection' as we may be doubtful about empirical events such as whether Winston Churchill sent a certain war telegram to Montgomery or not. Here is another logical impossibility. A person may 'doubt' the Empty Tomb, but all that can happen, and the worst that can happen, with the 'Resurrection' is that a person can be converted into infidelity; can lose that discernment-commitment we have discussed earlier. In this connection, we may notice how appropriate it is that in the examples William James gives of conversions into infidelity, the whole world is said to become 'flat' and to grow 'bleak' and 'cold'. For to talk of the world growing flat is to make the point that discernment ceases; to say that the world grows cold is to talk of ourselves as inactive and unresponsive. To disbelieve the Resurrection is, in this way, to be converted to infidelity. The truth of the Resurrection is logically integrated with our full commitment in Christ.

Incidentally, when people say that the Church is the best evidence of the Resurrection, the logical moves in this claim are two: (1) the Church is offered as something which evokes or expresses Christian commitment; (2) this commitment is then brought to the Resurrection narratives; whereupon (it would be claimed) the narratives can be organized as the loyalty of a lover can and will organize all the diverse facts which are a basis for the relation between himself and the beloved. The important practical point is that it is no use telling people that the Church is the best evidence for the Resurrection unless already not only do they acknowledge the existence of churches, but find that the Church evokes in them the kind of situation which must always be the empirical anchorage for a significant theology.

I need hardly say that these remarks on the Resurrection could continue for much longer, but I shall now conclude them by emphasizing how important it is to ask the right sort of questions about the Resurrection, and especially important not even to start discussing questions which imply that the Resurrection is what it could not be if the Christian claims for it were true.

We might notice in parenthesis that the same point might be made about 'Virgin Birth'. Here is another phrase whose logical structure must be suited to the kind of situation which is at the basis of the Christian religion. It is no use discussing the Virgin Birth as though it were no more than something which it cannot be if it is to be of distinctive Christian significance. It is no use taking 'Virgin Birth' as a description of something which can be settled once and for all as a matter of physiology and nothing else. Yet this is what has sometimes been done, even by Christian apologists of both liberal and conservative persuasions.

In an endeavour to face what have been thought to be the 'scientific' difficulties of the plain man, apologists have overlooked the oddness, the logical impropriety of the phrase. On the contrary, they have pleaded, it is a very scientific concept. Do we not know, it is argued, certain cases of parthenogenesis? Now I agree that this may be a useful *first* move towards recapturing, for an unbeliever, the significance of the phrase 'Virgin Birth'. 'After all "births" are not always all that straightforward', it might be said to the unbeliever, 'so you cannot have any final physiological hesitations about this doctrine. Indeed, there is this, that and the other physiological parallel.' But if an argument began in this way, it would seem to be most important and necessary, at the *second* move, to insist that the phrase 'Virgin Birth' is *not* one that can be given an exhaustive scientific placing. It is not a phrase which belongs to the language of Reproduction. The Virgin Birth is no more a matter of mere physiology than the Resurrection is a matter of a mere empty tomb. So do not let the alleged parallels of parthenogenesis deceive us, useful though they may be at certain early stages of Christian apologetic. If the Christian who believes in the Virgin Birth believes in parthenogenesis (and apparently some do and some do not) such parthenogenesis does not describe what is peculiarly distinctive about his belief. What is distinctive concerns something about the birth situation of Jesus which is *more than* its spatio-temporal features, however physiologically remarkable these may or may not have been.

Let us recognize that the doctrine of the Virgin Birth is essentially a claim for mystery at Christ's birth as at Christ's death. The birth was as much a situation spanning time and more, as was the Resurrection. Each exemplifies, though in different spatio-temporal terms, the same activity of God. From this standpoint it would follow that, while the birth of our Lord was from Mary's womb, Mary herself was no more active in the origination of our Lord than was Joseph. Indeed, I take it that this is the doctrine of 'conception by the Holy Spirit'. So we might conclude perhaps that the phrase 'Holy Spirit conception' makes the same point as is claimed by 'Virgin Birth', but in some ways makes it clearer and in a logically less misleading fashion.

After discussing the Crucifixion and the Resurrection—with this note on the Virgin Birth—we are well prepared for the Ascension. If I am right, here again was a significantly odd situation. But are not partings yet another example of the kind of situation we have tried to exemplify all along? We stand on the departure platform of a distant express and wave goodbye to a friend. There is an obvious sense in which the friend goes further and further away as the train departs, and in this sense his presence and significance grows clearly less and less. The details of clothes and face become less and less distinct; they first merge into the carriage, and the carriage into the general background, and the whole ultimately disappears into an area of steel grey mist, steam and blackness. But let us recall the story of the deepening darkness which we told in the first chapter. Just at that point, when all seems to merge in a dull uniformity, *a total negation*, can it not happen that there comes to us a disclosure of a constant presence? We know our friend to be with us in a way we had not realized before; we know a proximity and a presence which physical proximity and presence had somehow kept from us. Here then is a sense in which a *parting* can assure us of a *presence*.

Is not this a clue to the Ascension? Here was an odd situation indeed, which on the one hand had about it all the features of a departure; and yet it was a situation of high religious significance—a 'disclosure'—as well. How were the Apostles to understand it? Looking for model-language they found it in the Old Testament, and no doubt especially in the story of Elijah. Here also was a departure which was a disclosure, and it used ascension language as its currency. Perhaps we see here the equivalent for the ancient mind, of setting together the two words 'exit' and 'lift'; 'exit' and *ascenseur*. But neither the writers of the Old Testament nor of the New were concerned with the mechanics of the Ascension. They were not Waygoodotis experts. They had none of our contemporary interest in 'journeys into space'; they were no Jet Morgan fans. Rather, what they endeavoured to do was to understand an odd situation—a mystery —and for this purpose they took the Ascension model and qualified it. There was an 'ascension *into Heaven*', and the grammar will be less misleading if we speak of it as a '*heavenly* Ascension'. In such a case 'heavenly' would be the qualifier and 'Ascension' would be the model. There would be a series of departure terms: going, going, going . . . and the word 'heavenly' ensures that this series is never necessarily brought to an end, for however far we go—even to the top floor of the Empire State Building—we do not reach 'Heaven'. No doubt nowadays better than stories of either trains or lifts, would be stories of aircraft departure with the plane becoming increasingly 'lost' against the background of the sky. At any rate, in this way, to understand the kind of situation a Christian is talking about when he speaks of the Ascension, a departure story would have to be told, and continued, until there broke in on us just that kind of disclosure which comes to us when, as a friend in one obvious sense departs, there arises a new assurance of his continued presence with us.

But where has this brought us? Surely to the realization that doctrinally the Ascension is incomplete; that 'Ascension' is an incomplete symbol, that the situation which it evokes is a situation *not only* of departures *but also* of empowering, so that the 'Ascension' is logically completed only when we speak of the one event as 'Ascension=Pentecost', or at any rate of 'Ascension-empowering'. Not for the first time, and not for the last, do we see how *logically* misleading the *temporal* pegging of Christian doctrine may be, whatever its devotional usefulness.

Is it very rash to take this point one stage further? Let us look at the Ascension story in Acts.[1] We are told[2] that the two men who stood by the Apostles challenged them with the question: 'Why stand ye looking into Heaven?' On the face of it that would seem to be a natural question if it was intended to make the point that, after all, Jesus had gone, so that rather than waste their time hanging about and peering into the sky, the Apostles had better get back into Jerusalem. Indeed, it is often said that the intention was that the Apostles should wait at Jerusalem until, at Pentecost, the Holy Spirit initiated the Church.

But then let us notice that the two men had a further comment, which on the face of it makes their first question very odd, and strange indeed. They say: 'This Jesus which was received up from you into Heaven, shall so come in like manner as ye beheld him going into Heaven.'[3] Now, could not the Apostles immediately have retorted: 'Well, is not that the very best reason for stopping here to look? If Jesus is to come back precisely as we have just seen him go, and we expect him very soon, what could we do better than to stand here and look?' The verse is odd and no mistake. But rather than be puzzled by oddness, and then endeavour to get round it in some straightforward way, has not our approach suggested that oddness is *generally* a sign of logical impropriety? Before we try straightforward reductions, ought we not first to consider whether the address may not after all be *revealing*? I would not agree that the logic of theology can be reduced to that of poetry, but before anyone tries to iron out theological improprieties let him at any rate recall how silly it can be to try to eliminate even the oddness of poetry. How silly, for instance, to criticize Shelley's 'Ode

[1] Acts 1.6-11.   [2] Acts 1.11.   [3] Acts 1.11.

to the Skylark': 'Hail to thee blithe spirit, bird thou never wert', by complaining that it involves Shelley in self-contradiction. How silly to object that it is impossible to say of anything *both* that it is a skylark *and* not a bird. Even if the logic of theology is not identical with that of poetry, it is sufficiently like it in being odd; and our example has reminded us how silly it can be to try to eliminate the oddness of poetry. Caution, then, theologians!

What I suggest is that the challenge: 'Why stand ye looking into Heaven?' stands. This says, in effect, 'Why stand ye looking up at the sky?' You 'look', that is to say, yet you do not 'see'. You do not realize that 'this Jesus' which has been received up 'shall so come in like manner'. Now here is the crucial impropriety: the words *'so'* and *'in like manner'*— *both* phrases together. The 'so' of 'shall so come' has *the logical* point of emphasizing the coming, i.e. shall come, . . . come, . . . come . . . i.e. comes, and comes continually. And the manner?—well, have ye not beheld him going into Heaven? In other words, the two men say, 'have ye not seen him going, . . . going, . . . going . . . in that manner? He's come . . . so!'

On such an interpretation the challenge of the two men becomes: 'Realize that this Jesus is indeed coming and comes . . . precisely in this manner—in this "going away" which ye have beheld.' Here is an Ascension which is empowering as well.

Does this then conflict with the traditional account of Pentecost? At first sight perhaps it seems to do. Do we not imply that the Apostles were empowered, and the Church initiated before Pentecost? Certainly. But let us recall how Acts. 1.13 mentions explicitly the eleven Apostles, and how the rest of Chapter I of Acts is concerned with the replacement of Judas by Matthias so that the empty place may be filled. The fact that Matthias is elected to fill a vacancy and is then numbered with the Apostles, indicates that they are already very conscious that they have a 'ministry'. They are already interpreting their 'office' in terms of the Psalms. The Church, in short, has already emerged. What is distinctive about Pentecost is *not* that it started the Church; rather is Pentecost important as marking the beginning of its recorded public ministry.

Finally, as another approach to this idea of 'Ascension' as telling of some gradual departing process by means of which an empowering disclosure is evoked, let us recall that Westcott translates the verse in John 20.17 (commonly translated: 'I ascend unto my father and your father, and my God and your God') as 'I am ascending. . . .' In other words we might argue that (for Westcott) the Ascension tells of a departure which was no momentary event, but a departure of that gradual kind in whose gradualness, at some point or other, there comes an assurance of presence and an empowering. To help us to understand such a situation we have, as I have tried to show, empirical parallels well known to us in our own experience.

D. *'Son of Man'*

Let us first notice that though the phrase is obviously parallel *in grammar* to 'Son of God', there is no *logical* parallel whatever between them. It is logically impossible to give to each phrase the same kind of explicatory treatment. 'Son of God' is a phrase of which we shall say a little more in the next chapter. All that we need remark for the moment is that it is a phrase which is logically equivalent to 'Only Begotten Son', or 'Only Son', where all three phrases mean to identify that discernment-commitment which focuses on Jesus of Nazareth with that discernment-commitment in relation to which we posited—as would all theists and (say) the Jews in particular—the word 'God'. 'Son of Man', I suggest, is in its logical behaviour altogether different.

To see this, let us first go back to the rejection in the Patris of Mark 6, and parallels. Those who heard Jesus in the synagogue were astonished, and plainly puzzled, by his 'mighty works'.[1] But this impression passed, and we may rightly associate its passing with the application to Jesus of trade names and definite descriptions. 'Who is this?', asked his fellow-countrymen. The answer was 'the carpenter'[2], or 'the son of the carpenter'[2], or 'the son of Mary, and brother of James and Joses and Judas and Simon'.[2] Further, 'his sisters'[2] were well known. Here were ordinary general names, definite descriptions or trade names which, like 'Mr Justice Brown', 'the Crown', or 'the accused' in the language of the Law Courts, eliminate the depth from any situation. So it was that the 'prophet' was 'without honour'.[3] Familiarity had bred, if not contempt, at any rate spiritual blindness. His hearers were offended in Jesus, they missed his point, because they loved their ordinary language more than what exceeded it. So great was their love of the familiar language of straightforward classification and ordinary descriptive phrases, that his fellow countrymen soon professed unbelief rather than indulge in logical improprieties. Here again, like 'the gardener' in the Resurrection story, is the trade name, the impersonal reference, the verbal straitjacket which exhausts all the mystery and challenge from a situation.

Nor does that complete our comments. If we look at Mark 8 we shall realize that even the title 'The Messiah' = 'The Christ' is logically as unsatisfactory as any other definite description. It is commonly thought that the climax of Mark 8 comes with the Petrine confession at Caesarea Philippi: 'Thou art the Christ'.[4] But is this the climax? Jesus had asked: 'Who do men say that I am?'[5] and names had been proffered: 'John the Baptist', 'Elijah', 'One of the prophets'.[6] These were the names that others had given to him. But what were the names which the disciples would give him? Peter's answer is: 'The Christ'.[7] 'And he charged

---

[1] Mark 6.2.   [2] Mark 6.3.   [3] Mark 6.4.   [4] Mark 8.29.
[5] Mark 8.27.   [6] Mark 8.28.   [7] Mark 8.29.

them that they should tell no man of him'.[1] Or, I suppose,
'about it'. Now this verse has of course been customarily
incorporated into a theory of the Messianic Secret. But is it
not an important point that Chapter 8 immediately continues, *not* with our Lord's accepting Peter's description any
more than anybody else's description, but with his telling
them that the 'Son of Man'[2] must suffer many things?
Whatever we may think of Peter's earlier answer, it had
obviously *not* been the full story, nor anything like a notable
confession. Certainly there had been no full discernment
associated with the use of 'The Messiah' as a definite description. For Peter is rebuked for condemning what Jesus
himself has to say about the Son of Man's suffering and
resurrection.[3]

In other words, the phrase most suited to Jesus was apparently not 'The Messiah', but 'Son of Man'. But what then
is its logical currency? I suggest that its logic is like that of a
nickname, which we exemplified in Chapter I: a word
which has intrinsically the fewest possible empirical connections, but is very much filled out 'in use'. Further, in the
case of Jesus, there is an additional peculiarity that it is a
nickname given to himself by the person concerned. We may
think of it, then, like the child's nickname for himself—be it
Pim or Pom—and it is a well-known fact that it can be quite
a time before it dawns on the parent who the child is talking
of. May not this afford some clue to the logic of 'Son of Man'?

There are certainly four points which harmonize very
well with the supposition that it may do:

(a) I understand that all the evidence points in the
direction of our Lord using the phrase of himself; that this
phrase is that which our Lord himself used about himself.[4]

(b) Secondly, in our gospel narratives, 'Son of Man' can

---

[1] Mark 8.30.   [2] Mark 8.31.   [3] Mark 8.33.

[4] Except for John 12.34, the phrase as found in the Gospels is only
used by Jesus; and John 12.34 presupposes its use by Jesus.

often work like 'I'; it can often be logically synonymous with 'I'. This is plain if we recall the work of historical critics who showed that very often this substitution was, or may have been, made.[1]

(c) Neither has the phrase any clear theological setting. It is true that we may find a token of the phrase in Enoch or Daniel; it is equally true that in Aramaic it may mean no more than just 'man'. In other words, while it has admittedly some empirical connections, it is a phrase which is beautifully problematical,[2] and while it is obviously interesting to discover its uses in other connections—in the Old Testament, and in the Apocrypha, for example—yet if I am right, the apologist would compromise his Christianity and his claims for Jesus of Nazareth if he gave the phrase, as used by Jesus himself, any sort of final exact setting outside the pages of the New Testament. It must gain its Christian meaning 'in use'.

(d) Finally, on this view, taking the analogy of the parents

[1] E.g. in Mark 9.27 ('I'), Luke 9.18 ('I') or Matt. 16.13 ('I, the Son of Man'; or 'Son of Man' alone).

[2] Cp. H. Lietzmann: *Der Menschensohn*, where he discusses the phrase 'Son of Man' in Aramaic and concludes that in Galilean Aramaic the expression is 'the most colourless and indeterminate designation of human individual'—so much so that it works very like an indefinite pronoun. Nor did the 'fresh and very thorough examination of the linguistic evidence' carried out by P. Fibig in 1901 essentially alter the particular conclusion we have taken from Lietzmann. For further details, see the section 'Son of Man' in *Dictionary of Christ and the Gospels*, ed. J. Hastings, from which this reference is taken. It might be said, however, that Mowinckel has shown in *He that Cometh* (1956) that 'Son of Man' has a much firmer setting in the descriptive language of the times than has hitherto for the most part been supposed, that it was not (as we have suggested) delightfully problematical. But even if that were true, it would *not* follow that we can rightly regard the phrase as straightforwardly descriptive. Indeed, it would *still* have to have a peculiar logic if it was to be a religious phrase.

The difference (if Mowinckel were correct) would be that this logical peculiarity would not be so visible to the naked eye. We should be back to the general case where ordinary syntax conceals rather than reveals logical syntax; whereas in the text not the least interest of 'Son of Man' is that it is a phrase for whose odd logical placing we are prepared from the outset.

and the child, we may perhaps better understand why the disciples were so puzzled about our Lord.[1]

It is some time before the puzzled parents realize who Pim is, though one way and another they have learned meanwhile quite a deal about him. The realization eventually comes in some 'disclosure' which reveals at one and the same time not only who Pim is—'why, it's our eldest boy after all!'—but at once transfers to him the picture they have meanwhile been building up. Before that 'disclosure' Pim might have been any one of four or five children, but not so now. Now they know Pim, and this means that they 'know' their 'eldest boy' all the better.

So were the disciples puzzled by the Crucifixion, and even at first by the Resurrection: for though these events had always been associated with the 'Son of Man' the disciples had not realized that this was a phrase which distinctively characterized, as a nickname, one whom they had known by the traditional descriptive title of 'Messiah'. It was only after the 'disclosure' that the parents associated with him whom they had known all along as 'our eldest boy' all the escapades that they had come to associate with Pim.

Actually, we may take a rather more complex example to illustrate this puzzlement of the disciples, in so far as it centres around an uncertainty of title, and the enigma of what is logically like a nickname.

Suppose that a school in some remote part of the Scottish Highlands has been without a Headmaster for quite a long time; but one is expected to arrive any day. Whereupon a certain man arrives who takes immediate charge of the school, and while he does not expressly claim to be the Headmaster, he allows others to use the title of himself. At the same time, when he is making public announcements, he always uses some phrase like *Praepositus*. For example, the boys are told: '*Praepositus* has decided that the school will

[1] Compare the crowd in John 12.34: 'Who is this Son of Man?'

have a fortnight's holiday from next Monday': '*Praepositus* has decided that henceforward lunch shall be 2*s*. 9*d*.'; '*Praepositus* will attend a garden party for parents and friends next Saturday', and so on. Now suppose that on such occasions as this last one, he who was called 'the Headmaster' always turned up, but never anyone who claimed *explicitly* to be *Praepositus*. Plainly, there would be great uncertainty and puzzlement. The 'Headmaster' might be *Praepositus* or he might not. . . .

But suppose now that on a certain day, this man, supposedly 'the Headmaster' for certain, and only problematically *Praepositus* behaved in a way that was utterly and entirely contrary to the traditional notions of headmastership, e.g. he proceeded to arrange for the school's demolition, the immediate reaction of the parents would be one of shock and bewilderment. But they then discover that hitherto unknown to them, a new and altogether better school has already been built but a short distance away, and that *Praepositus* is their generous benefactor. In these circumstances they might well say: 'We were wrong after all in thinking of him as "the Headmaster", but we see now who *Praepositus* is, and what is distinctive about him. *Praepositus* is our benefactor's name for himself, and his demolition of the school is only part of his generous scheme of reorganization.'

Notice that the situation which settled his being *Praepositus* and revealed also what was distinctively praeposital, also made it impossible for the man to be 'the Headmaster' in the traditional sense.

May not this story—crude though it be—illuminate to some degree the puzzlement of the disciples? Here was a person who never actually claimed to be 'the Messiah' though he allowed others on occasion to use the title of him. On the other hand, he talked very often of 'Son of Man' but never *explicitly* claimed that title either. No wonder there was uncertainty and puzzlement. He was never netted by the titles with which *they* were familiar; and *he* also used a title whose meaning and reference they could not altogether understand.[1] Then came the Crucifixion. Their immediate reaction was one of shock and bewilderment. They realized so very clearly that they had been mistaken all along about the one description of the man they had supposed incorrigible. For 'crucifixion' had no place in the traditional 'Messiah' language. 'Crucifixion' was a linguistic stumbling block to Jewish language about a Messiah. But the event which made it impossible for this person to be 'Messiah' in the traditional sense, was soon followed by and integrally connected with another event, and both events had always found a place in 'Son of Man' language, e.g. 'the Son of Man must suffer many things and be killed, and after three days rise again'.[2]

So did the Crucifixion-Resurrection not only settle his being 'Son of Man', but also revealed what was distinctively covered by that phrase. When the light dawned and the penny dropped, 'Messiah' had to become 'crucified and risen Messiah'—a logical impropriety indeed—before it could even claim to be appropriate currency for a phrase equivalent to 'Son of Man', whose full significance was now, and for the first time, seen. So significant indeed was this phrase that it was rarely used again.[3] For it had proved to be a phrase used by Jesus to name himself. To the disciples it must have been as sacred as, indeed more sacred than, the *Tetragrammaton* of the Jews. This is perhaps one reason why, despite the possibility of logical pitfalls, traditional theology has spoken more readily of the 'risen Christ' than of the 'Son of Man'. The fact that 'Son of Man' was Jesus' own name for himself may not be the only reason for this

[1] Cp. Westcott: *Gospel of St John*, pp. 33ff. 'It was essentially a new title . . .'

[2] Mark 8.31.

[3] The use by St Stephen at martyrdom is probably the only recorded instance of its explicit application to Jesus: Acts 7.56.

preference, but it is no doubt one reason, and an important one at that.

E. *Miracle Language*

Here is our last example of logical impropriety in the Bible; last, but not least important. For it is certainly a major feature of the biblical narrative. If indeed we are looking for logical improprieties in the Bible, miracle language can never be ignored. What then is the logical structure of miracle language? What is a miracle? Our answer must start from the point that a miracle is a non-conforming event, a *miraculum* whose non-conformity, whose oddness, evokes, gives rise to, what we have called a characteristically theological situation. With a miracle, a situation 'comes alive', the light dawns, the penny drops.

To express this nonconformity people have spoken of a miracle as a 'breach of natural law'. But taken literally, such language has no sort of significance. Scientific laws are always being broken, and they are as easily mended. For instance, take the inverse square law of gravitation which at one time seemed to be a law which never could be broken. According to this law, the orbits of the planets would be ellipses. But in due course it was found that the orbit of Mercury was *not* an accurate ellipse. After tracing almost an ellipse the planet just fails to reach, at the end of one revolution, the point from which it has started on that revolution. The upshot was that the Newtonian inverse square law was modified by the introduction of a further term relating to inverse cubes. All that was talked of by the old gravitational law, was talked of by the new law—and much else besides. The first law had been broken (if we wish to speak thus), but only to be replaced at once by a second.

The same is true about the gas equation: $PV = RT$. This seems to be an accurate generalization on most occasions. But at low pressure, when the volume is small, the law is 'broken'. But it is as easily mended, and we have the van der Waals correction: $\left(P + \frac{a}{V^2}\right)$ $(V-b) = RT$. In other words, there is apparently no special significance about a 'broken law'.

Certainly the phrase cannot be significant if it has a straightforward structure, and belongs to the logic of science. What structure then must it have, and what sort of event will it talk about, if it successfully tells a theological tale? Once again the phrase 'breach of natural law' can be taken as a *qualified model*. 'Natural law' is a model from the natural sciences, and 'breach' is a qualifying operator. What we are then directed to do is to consider a law, and then to contemplate circumstances which will break it, till this law passes into another, whereupon the process is repeated. The result is that we have the sequence: law, break, reformulate, break, reformulate, break . . . and the story must continue until there dawns on us a characteristically religious situation, and with it the conviction that a scientific law, no matter how often reformulated, never gives of such a situation an exhaustive description.

But what does 'miracle' tell us about such a situation? What particular claim do we make about a characteristically religious situation evoked in this way when we call it a *miracle*? To answer these questions let us look at some examples of miracle language. When we do, we shall find that in a miracle story 'God' has been inserted into a language-frame from which a 'person' word has been deleted. Miracle stories are thus stories of characteristically personal activity, with 'God' substituted for a person-word, as the following examples show:

(a) The most characteristically personal activity is human reproduction. So we have stories of miraculous' births, e.g. Genesis 21.1: Sarah giving birth to Isaac.

(b) Or again, the making of fires and smoke must have been, at once time, a very characteristic personal activity.

So it is that the presence of the fire and cloud exhibits the presence of God in Ex. 13.21 and 22.

(c) Again, personal activity shows itself characteristically in the production of satisfying and appropriate food. Not unnaturally then, we have the manna of Ex. 16.14-35; the cruse of oil and barrel of meal of I Kings 17.8-16; or a hundred men being fed with five loaves, II Kings 4.42-44.

(d) Further, the creation of novelty in an otherwise regular environment can exhibit personal activity and power—the production of light after dark; the floating of iron ships on water; the piling up of water in dams. Hence it is that these features when no person is present, bespeak God's miraculous power and activity, exhibited in terms of a particular personal concern—Joshua 10.12; II Kings 20.9-11; II Kings 6.5-7; Ex. 14.21.

(e) Unfortunately personal power is only too often shown in warfare and the use of warlike weapons. Hence a bow in the cloud could bespeak the personal activity of God—the rainbow of Gen. 9.13.

(f) What could exhibit personal power more than control and direction by the hand? So it is that we read in I Sam. 5.11, of the 'hand of the Lord' being very heavy on the Philistines when the Ark of the God of Israel was with them.

What a miracle claims about the universe is, then, that on some occasion the universe 'comes alive' in a personal sort of way. It is as though, day after day for years, a ticket examiner at the station has impressed us by his machine-like efficiency, reversing our ticket, clipping it at the appropriate point, enumerating our destination, and naming the platform and time of our train, and all with the routine precision of a complex machine. Then, one day, we book a ticket to a certain remote village which proves to be the very spot where he was born, and which he has not seen since a child. In naming our destination today, there is still the routine answer with machine-like precision, but there is maybe an oddity of pronunciation, maybe a quiver in the voice; but in any event our 'eyes meet' and we think to ourselves: 'By jove, he is human after all.' An impersonal situation comes alive in a characteristically personal sort of way, there is 'more' to it than on earlier occasions, and we have a situation reminiscent of a miracle. Notice that we need not deny that scientific precision language could be used about a miraculous situation. But what is needed is some other language *as well*, which will be appropriate currency for the 'more'. Alongside, and along with, the precision language must go an odder language which witnesses to the fact that the situation is *only in part* perceptual, and it will be this odder language which in the case of a miracle, talks about the 'more', about what is distinctively religious, *in personal terms*.

In this way, we may see 'miracle' and 'free will' as logical parallels. Each claims a 'personal' situation which needs *more than* scientific language to talk about it. 'Free will' does not deny determinism any more than it *necessarily implies* indeterminism; rather it claims a characteristically 'personal' situation which the language of causal connectedness never exhausts. So with a 'miracle' situation: it neither denies nor asserts the applicability of the language of scientific law to the spatio-temporal features it contains, but it claims that such language never tells the full story. It thus claims about the *objective* features of a certain situation what free-will claims about the *subjective* features of other situations: it makes (we may say) a 'free-will' claim about the Universe.

So far we have taken as examples none but Old Testament miracles, but we might say equally about the miracles of the New Testament, that they display a power which is also a personal concern. Plainly this is so with the miracles of healing and of feeding—the draughts of fishes, the water into wine. In all these cases the Universe came alive in a way which displayed personal concern. But are there not exceptions? Are there not some New Testament miracles which less obviously bespeak personal concern? There are perhaps three on which a comment is worth while:

(i) *The Temple tax for two found in the fish's mouth.*[1] Even here it might be asserted that the miracle displayed the personal concern of God, that provided even for the payment of Temple dues.

(ii) *The raising of Lazarus.*[2] It might be said that this is obviously a miracle of personal concern—are not Martha and Mary quite distracted by the death of their brother, and does not the raising of Lazarus meet their heart-felt personal need? That may be so, and if it is the case, there is nothing exceptional about this miracle. But in this case two further reflections are possible:

(a) If we regard the miracle as one which exhibits a personal concern—see verses 33, 35 and 38—we must, I think, recognize that it is, however, only demanded because Mary and Martha failed to realize and acknowledge the full truth of the Christian gospel. For the light had not dawned at the crucial point. Martha and Mary did *not* see the point of the proclamation by Jesus: 'I am the Resurrection and the Life'.[3] Only thereafter did the actual miracle of the raising of Lazarus occur.

(b) Again, whether the miracle tells of a personal concern or not, it may *also* have a wider significance. May it not anticipate the Resurrection of Jesus in the same way that the birth of John the Baptist anticipates the Birth of Jesus; each predecessor, in its own way, pointing forward to make clearer the uniqueness of what is claimed about our Lord himself? His Birth is that of John the Baptist *plus*; his Resurrection is the raising of Lazarus *plus*.

(iii) Finally—*the cursing of the fig tree.*[4] Perhaps from the present point of view this is *prima facie* the most important

---

[1] Matt. 17.27.   [2] John 11.1-44.
[3] John 11.25.   [4] Mark 11.12.

exception to our generalization that New Testament miracles always bespeak a personal concern.

It is not part of our present purpose to examine the text of any narrative in detail, or to discuss the likelihood of particular incidents having occurred. Those are tasks we have not now set ourselves, though they are tasks which would have to be included in any full treatment of miracles. What, for our purpose, is important about the cursing of the fig tree is that here, if it happened, would be a 'miracle' which displayed nothing but sheer power—a power which apparently exhibits no characteristically personal activity, no personal concern—a power which is wholly exhaustible in terms of spatio-temporal events. To the philosopher's eye, therefore, apart from any textual critique, there is reason to think of this 'miracle' in a different category altogether from those we have otherwise mentioned. It is, to the philosopher, a miracle-story where there does not seem to be any characteristically personal activity, anything which is personally elusive. So far as the New Testament is concerned, this miracle is in a class by itself. Not surprisingly, then, have commentators shown themselves puzzled by this incident. Not surprisingly have some even gone so far as to remark how closely it can be paralleled with the miracle-stories in the Apocryphal Gospels.

This is certainly what we would expect on philosophical grounds. Philosophically, the cursing of the fig tree describes a situation of very different status from the other New Testament miracles.

As for the miracles concerning our Lord's own life and person, we have already said something about these, and need now say no more. I will merely conclude by recalling that, as we would expect, a miracle-story in general tells of a 'disclosure'; of a characteristically theological situation; of a situation which had 'depth' and 'mystery'; a situation which is more than 'what is seen'. About such a situation, a miracle-story makes a special and particular claim, viz. that in it is exhibited a 'personal invervention' (compare how we speak of free-will situations), a 'power' which is a 'personal concern'. So we may say summarily that miracle-stories are endeavours in terms of public language to express the fact that certain situations possess observable factors of a non-personal kind which by their odd pattern are nevertheless expressive of characteristically personal activity. In a miracle the Universe declares itself personal at a point where persons are not; and the miracle story must be odd enough to make this remarkable claim. We shall never measure the logic of miracle stories by reading them off against scientific assertions; the point they make is one very different from any which can be made in scientific language.

IV

CHRISTIAN LANGUAGE

2. THE LANGUAGE OF CHRISTIAN DOCTRINE

In the first chapter I argued that as compared with 'what's seen' and our appropriate attitude thereto, the characteristically religious situation—characterized by a 'discernment-commitment'—was nothing if not odd. I then gave examples to illustrate that claim, showing at the same time that the currency for such an odd situation would have to be suitably odd language.

In the second chapter I took certain traditional phrases used about God, and showed how their logical behaviour was indeed suited to the kind of situation we had claimed as the basis of all religious language. Further, I showed that to neglect the logical complexity of such phrases inevitably gave rise to confusion and misunderstandings which showed themselves in all kinds of unnecessary puzzles and problems.

In the last chapter I showed that the language of the Bible, too, had an odd structure suited to its theme. It was neither science nor history, and the merit of Bultmann was to remind us that the Bible was about something odd, and in part elusive—which is what religious situations in fact are. Here is the Bible as 'the Word of God'. The Bible is *not* the 'words of God', which a slight grammatical variant might suggest, but its 'words' make the light to dawn, make situations come alive, evoke that kind of situation which demands the word 'God'.

We next took some particular examples. I showed how the logic of naming could illuminate the Hebrew hesitation to name God; how the 'name' of Ex. 3 was very appropriately and as we would expect, a tautology whose logic the revisers concealed when they tried to make an assertion from it, as they did in marginal notes.

We then saw how prophetic language worked as disclosure language; and we explained what would be meant on this basis by the 'fulfilment' of prophecy, noting as a consequence that there would be important *logical* differences between language which was apocalyptic, and language appropriate to Christian fulfilment.

Turning then to the New Testament, and first by reference to the ending of Mark, followed by the story of the Samaritan woman, I tried to show how the New Testament contrives to express and evoke a situation distinctively religious. Further, we saw that far from the Cross, the Resurrection and the Ascension being properly understood respectively as a good plain historical event, something a shade puzzling, and something quite extraordinary, all three are incorporated in the Christian dispensation *only if* they are all situations of the kind we have had in mind throughout this book—situations which are never merely a Crucifixion or the discovery of an Empty Tomb, or a display of levitation.

As for the phrase 'Son of Man', I suggested that we might see this as a phrase used by our Lord himself which was problematical in its logic, and gained its meaning in use, so that it was logically like the nickname by which a child puzzles his parents until 'the light dawns' and they understand.

Finally, we considered the language of miracles as a particular expression of biblical impropriety. We saw that miracle language takes the language of some characteristically personal activity, often one which shows itself in a concern for the welfare of humanity, and uses such language of situations where however—and hence the impropriety—no human being is signified. There is no need to deny that scientific

152

language as well as miracle language can be used of such situations. For scientific language has a different story to tell about these situations; nor by this time of day need there be any difficulty in our having to admit that one situation may be tractable in terms of languages which fall into two distinct logical areas.

Once or twice we came near to suggesting that the language of *Christian* miracles exhibits a *double* impropriety; bespeaks a *special* kind of characteristically personal situation.[1] This in fact is what the Christian would claim. He would claim that the religious situations to which he appeals exhibit a distinctive uniqueness. He would agree that unless Christian stories exhibit this *double* dose of impropriety they will never tell their *full* tale. The Christian claim is obviously centred on 'disclosure' situations where the penny drops, the light dawns; where there breaks in on us a situation characteristically different from its immediate predecessors. But the Christian goes further in appealing to situations which, while of this kind, are also, amongst such situations, distinctive and unique.

The empirical basis of Christian doctrine is always to be sought in such *distinctive and unique* 'disclosure' situations, and in this last chapter we shall see how, in their logical behaviour, its characteristic assertions are suited to such a distinctive basis as this. Let us begin by noting that Christian doctrine first arose from a natural desire to acquaint others with what the earliest convert believed to be a 'disclosure' situation of a unique and distinctive kind; to confront others with what had to them been so revolutionary and important. To do this it was necessary to evoke the all-important situation by means of language already familiar to prospective converts. Here then was a major problem at the outset: how to evoke a distinctive and unique disclosure in terms of language which, even if it had been suited to 'disclosure' situations in

[1] Cp., e.g., pp. 118-21 and 147-8.

the past, had no unique character about it? The earliest evangelists met this difficulty in a rough and ready way, by taking as many traditional phrases as they could, and mixing them in the most riotous manner possible. This primitive stage we find in the early speeches of Acts. Notice, for instance, the various logical areas into which the phrases used in the early speeches of St Peter, naturally fall: 'God hath glorified his *servant* (*child*) Jesus whom ye delivered up. . . . Ye denied *the Holy* and *the Righteous One* . . . and killed the *Prince* (*Author*) *of life* whom God raised from the dead.'[1] Or again: 'God hath made him *both Lord* and *Christ*, this Jesus whom ye crucified.'[2] Or: 'Jesus whom ye slew, hanging him on a tree . . . him did God exalt with his right hand to be *a Prince* and *a Saviour* for to give repentance to Israel, and remission of sins.'[3] Jesus! Spoken of as God's servant, child, Christ, Lord; as the Holy and Righteous One; as Saviour, Prince, and Author of Life; as raised from the dead.

What a riotous mixture of phrases this is, belonging intrinsically to so many different logical areas with a diversity even greater than that of the Old Testament. This riotous mixing is in effect a rough and ready attempt to secure that special logical impropriety needed to express the Christian message. Each word is logically qualified by the presence of the others, and in this way each word comes to display a suitable measure of impropriety. I am not saying, for a moment, that St Peter explicitly gave his subject this kind of logical structure; that he deliberately constructed it with such a logical plan in mind.[4] What I am saying is that because the speech of St Peter succeeded (where it did), we ourselves can in fact discern such a logical complexity in the speech now. But St Peter's concern was first and foremost to evoke the distinctive Christian situation, and the logical behaviour of his words did not at all interest him. Here was

---

[1] Acts 3.13, 14, 15. [2] Acts 2.36. [3] Acts 5.30, 31.
[4] Cp. my remarks on pp. 91-2, Chapter III.

the *Kerygma*, the preaching, and its whole point was to evoke an appropriate situation of challenge and response. It is true that if we scan the various phrases of which we have given some examples above, to see if there is any general pattern to which they all conform, we might say that their general claim was that 'God did something through Jesus', and that such an assertion as this gives the general structure to which the *Kerygma* conformed. But with the *Kerygma* there was no attempt to rationalize or expound or discuss the fact which is preached and proclaimed. What was of over-riding importance was to evoke the situation, and little did it matter at this stage what language was used to do that. The language might be 'near-gibberish'—'speaking with tongues'. So far, we had indeed no *doctrine* as such. But before long people began to have difficulties.

To the Greeks, what was being said kerygmatically, was foolishness: Could there be anyone of whom both the words 'God' and 'man' had to be used? Their metaphysical maps left no place for such a logical geography of 'Jesus'. The Jews had their own stumbling block: there was no place for 'Crucifixion' in what they wanted to say about 'Messiah'. In other words, neither Jews nor Greeks could formulate a credible language in which this preaching could be expressed. Nor were the difficulties only from without; there were internal troubles as well. Here were orthodox Jews who for years had regularly recited the *Shema*: 'Hear, O Israel, the Lord our God is one Lord'. What, then, had they to say of the relationship of Jesus to God? In this way, and for various reasons, Christianity had to show how what it wished to say, was related to the great systems of Greek thought on the one hand and Jewish traditional teaching on the other. Christianity had to investigate the logical structure of the *Kerygma*. Preaching had to become analysis and teaching. Here was the start of Christian doctrine.

The problem of Christian doctrine then was in principle,

one of systematizing what we have called the riotous mixture of phrases which had characterized the *Kerygma*. Christian doctrine had to produce some sort of consistent scheme against which these various phrases could be read off; some background framework of ideas against which their logical edges could be aligned, and their appropriate claims made evident. So Christian doctrine began by bringing alongside these various phrases some interpretative rule which might be as abstract and general as some dominant metaphysical idea, or as concrete as some particular relationship. Among the most famous of these interpretative ideas were the model of sonship, and the metaphysical idea of *Logos*.[1] Sometimes both the idea and the model were used by the same theologian, as in the case of Origen. It was as though the general pattern of the kerygmatic phrases was taken to be, as we have suggested; 'God did something through Jesus', this general pattern being then translated according to some appropriate model or idea, whereupon (for example) 'God sent his *Son*' or 'the Word (*Logos*) became flesh', become illuminating pictures by which to *understand* and expound what the *Kerygma* had proclaimed.

Here is the kind of approach which logical empiricism would make to Christian doctrine, and to see the approach in rather greater detail, let us look briefly at each of these translations in turn.

1. *'God sent his Son'*

Here was a picture, then, meant to illuminate the riotous mixture of kerygmatic phrases; a pictorial interpretation

[1] I am aware, of course, of the importance of 'Philonism' as such an 'interpretative rule', and whether or not we ascribe to it the over-riding importance which Wolfson does in his *Philosophy of the Church Fathers* (Harvard and O.U.P., 1956), I entirely agree that, in principle, *some* sort of rule or rules was brought alongside the medley of Christian phrases so as to effect their logical mapping. But I would differ from Wolfson in various ways whose discussion is beyond the scope of this book, and of which the reader may gain an inkling from my review in *Philosophical Quarterly*.

designed for the better *understanding* of what the riotous mixture evoked and proclaimed. But to provide a better understanding was to provide also new difficulties. Admitting
that this idea of Sonship illuminates the general pattern we
have discerned in the *Kerygma*, the trouble was that with the
illumination came also (as so often happens) a puzzlement
which had not occurred before. In this puzzlement, as a
leading problem, was the question: Does the assertion: 'God
sent his Son', mean that God is to be altogether distinguished
from, and be apart from, his Son? Granted that we wish to
use the model of 'sonship', are not some precautions necessary? Must we not guard against any suggestion of subordination? Jesus must not be 'subordinated' to God, so as
to compromise his divinity. How, though, can we be sure
that this misunderstanding is avoided?

Now, if a person of philosophical temperament approached
this idea of sonship—and Origen may be taken as an example
of such a case—he might argue (to avoid the misunderstanding) that whenever we talk of a 'son' we imply that there is
a father; that 'son' logically necessitates 'father'.[1] 'Son' and
'Father' are thus connected by a logical necessity. Now
when Origen and others speak of the 'eternal generation of
the Son', here is a phrase meant to make this point of a
logically necessary connection, though it makes it (we may
think unfortunately) in the material mode. However, to
someone like Origen, the picture of Sonship, when qualified
by the phrase 'eternal generation' could avoid any charge of
subordination.

But to start on doctrine at all is to give hostages to fortune.
As soon as one difficulty seems to be settled, another arises.
For how (it is asked) can a 'son' be 'eternally generated'? On
the face of it this seems a nonsense question. To counter it,
two points must be made:

(i) We must first recall that the doctrine of the eternal

[1] 'No one can be a father without having a son' (*de Principiis*, i. 2. 10).

generation expresses an important logical point misleadingly in the material mode. The doctrine of eternal generation is not a super-scientific theory of organic development; we can, for example, ask no significant questions about the rate of generation: $\dfrac{\text{`d}G\text{'}}{\text{d}t}$. 'Power is now being continually generated', when asserted by the Chairman of the Central Electricity Authority on opening a new Station, has no logical kinship whatever with 'The Son is eternally generated' when asserted by the Chairman of a Patristic Conference as he opens his paper. In speaking of the 'eternal generation of the Son', we are not talking about what goes on at all times in some sort of heavenly laboratory, or labour-ward.

(ii) The doctrine then is a logical safeguard, not a super-scientific assertion. Is there however an alternative and independent way of expressing its logical point? Let our minds recall the apparent nonsense questions that people have asked about First Cause and Creation *ex nihilo*, when they have thought of these as super-scientific curiosities. May it not be that (taking a hint from earlier discussions) 'eternal generation of the Son' is in principle a qualified model? In this case, 'Son's generation' gives a model situation, a situation which tells of the kinship between a father and his son. This situation is then developed by the qualifier 'eternal', so that we talk of closer and closer kinship, greater and greater intimacy, until there is evoked a worshipful situation of disclosure, in relation to which the two terms 'God' and 'the Son' find their usage. Further, it would now be claimed that such a disclosure situation duplicates the kind of worshipful disclosure which occurred to those who found themselves in the presence of Jesus of Nazareth. Finally, we might recall that once again 'eternal generation' no more talks of a sort of generation than 'infinite sum' specifies a sort of sum; both are means of specifying the very complex logical geography of certain symbols. In this case, the symbol with a very complex logical geography is 'the Son'.

Along such lines would be the possibility of discussion with those who alleged that the doctrine of eternal generation was nonsense. Rather is it to be seen as illuminating impropriety. But such a man as Arius had no tongue for logical improprieties. He was (we might say) a plain man who wanted to speak plainly. In effect Arius said: 'Sons come after fathers', so that if we are to talk about Jesus in terms of sonship, we cannot escape some degree of subordination if we are to use words meaningfully. So did Arius idolize what is only a model, and run it to death. It is true that he tried to make the subordination minimal; but some subordination he had to have to safeguard what seemed to him the meaning of the words. Hence, there must be at least 'once when he was not': ἦν πότε ὅτε οὐκ ἦν. Arius could not see how to preserve the intelligibility of his Christology and at the same time to have less subordination than this. He did not realize that the words he was using about God and Jesus would *not* fit their subject at every point; that this is logically inevitable if 'God' and 'Jesus' mean what Christians have meant them to mean. Arius did not realize that words like 'son' and 'father' only provided models. At the same time, let us readily recognize that the orthodox, from their side, were far from being clear what they were doing in qualifying such models.

For instance when orthodoxy claims, as it did at Nicea, that the Son is 'of one substance with the Father', here is no kind of super-scientific discovery. Here is a traditional metaphysical category—'substance'—a category which inevitably has a strange tale to tell. It is a classical qualifier, born to the job. For its professional purpose is to call attention to something or other which (it claims) unites certain empirical criteria, but about which these criteria do not themselves tell the whole truth, though they tell an important part of it. 'Substance' is a word which is quite accustomed to come alongside straightforward picture words to tell a fuller story, and to talk of what unites them despite their diversity.[1] It can therefore be a useful word for providing an appropriate qualification to any father-son picture when the intention is to emphasize the inadequacy of the picture in so far as it implies separable terms. In this way 'of one substance' becomes a logical kinsman with 'eternal generation', and both are phrases meant to maintain a logically necessary connection between 'God' and 'Jesus' despite the use of a father-son model by plain men. So *Homo-ousion* Orthodoxy was once again qualifying the father-son relationship in such a way that it became suitable currency for the relation between God and Jesus of Nazareth: and such qualification, as we have seen, demanded words and phrases whose logical behaviour was as complex as that of 'substance' and 'eternal generation'.

How necessary, then, to recognize the logical complexity of Christian claims before we argue about them; before we discuss their truth and falsity. As we have already suggested, not even orthodoxy always recognized the complexity of the claim it was making, and we may illustrate that point by taking our example one stage further and at the same time offering the promised interpretation of the phrase 'Son of God'.[2] For orthodoxy to speak of Jesus as 'Son of God' may be regarded (from one philosophical point of view) as an insistence that 'son' could be used of 'Jesus' if it was qualified; and we have seen that orthodoxy was right in so insisting, as against Arius, that when it used the word 'son', it was using it with becoming impropriety. '*Son* of God' thus becomes a shorthand version of '*Son* eternally generated from God' or '*Son* of one substance with God'. So far, so good. But orthodoxy also talked of Jesus as a son who was '$\mu o \nu o \gamma \epsilon \nu \acute{\eta} s$'; that is, an 'only child'. Here was another way of expressing

---

[1] An apple is, e.g., such 'distinct perceptions'—it is bitter, hard, green, red and yellow—but as 'one thing' it has (the traditional story goes) a uniting, underlying 'substance'.

[2] See p. 137, above.

the uniqueness of Jesus, of qualifying such a model as 'Son' or 'child'. But it is quite plain that the logical complexity of this assertion might well be overlooked. 'Only son' might well seem to be saying no more than that Jesus had at least no brothers and perhaps no sisters. How many of the discussions of Mark 6.3 (for example) have implicitly been working along these lines? But does the uniqueness Christians have wished to claim for Christ disappear if Christ had any brothers or sisters, if he was not *in a literal and straightforward sense* an 'only child'? For this phrase only expresses the unique claim Christians wish to make if it is a logical impropriety; if 'only' is a logical kinsman of 'eternally generated'; and 'of one substance'.

So we may say that it was an inspired ambiguity that began to translate μονογενής by both *unicus* and *unigenitus*, so that we have as English alternatives 'Only Son' and 'Only-begotten Son'. For once people began to speak of an 'only begotten Son' they might remember that they had also spoken of an 'eternally begotten Son', and the risk of literalism about 'only son' would be avoided. If they then spoke of Jesus as God's 'only Son' they would not be likely to think of Jesus as an 'only child' but rather (in the expanded phrase) as an 'only begotten Son', which might thereafter and of course be equally translated 'eternally generated Son'; the point being that, in these phrases, 'only' and 'eternally' would have the same logical placings. Then, though in a shorthand way, we might write of Jesus as 'God's Only Son', we would not be tempted to suppose that 'Only Son', because simple in grammar, is simple in its logical behaviour. On the contrary, as we have tried to show, 'Only Son' is a phrase of high logical complexity. 'Only Son' = 'Only begotten Son' = 'Eternally begotten Son' = 'Eternally generated Son' = 'Only Son of God', and none of these are straightforward phrases, but in each case there is the same *model* which has been given various *qualifications*, all of a complex kind.

2. Let us now glance very briefly at a second example of the kind of approach which logical empiricism makes to Christian doctrine, by recalling how *Logos* was used as a metaphysical idea to systematize the riotous mixture of phrases used in the early preaching. The great merit of this concept was that it enabled people to talk in philosophical terms of both similarity and difference, and this is what they wished to do about God and Jesus. A 'word' is obviously other than the speaker; it also is intimately associated with him—'he is as good as his word'. Here then was a concept which, if people were wishing to illuminate the relation between God and Jesus, might be of great usefulness, and it was all the better for being a key word in various 'metaphysical' schemes, e.g. that of Philo.

For our present purpose, all that we need notice is that there were two phrases to express this double standpoint of *Logos*. There was an immanent *Logos* (ἐνδιάθετος) where word and speaker were intimately connected, and a *Logos* proceeding forth in various operations (προφορικός) where word and speaker were separated. The danger was, of course, that this second aspect of *Logos* might be emphasized too strongly, whereupon the *Logos* model could land its adherents into as unsatisfactory a subordinationism as did sonship. To guard against this it was essential once again to use qualifying phrases such as 'co-eternity' and 'inseparable union' and in this same logical setting comes the traditional phrase 'eternal procession' as used of the *Logos*. But here again is a qualified model. What is now being asserted is that the 'going forth' which quite straightforwardly characterizes words as they are uttered, must, when this model is used of the relation of Jesus to God, be so qualified (and is by 'eternal') as to make it equally plain that in this case 'going forth' implies no sort of separation, no sort of gap, no sort of subordination. On this view 'eternal' will qualify 'procession' something like 'continuous' can qualify certain mathematical functions. If we take two values of a 'continuous' function, then however near they be together, there is always a value between. The procedure may be repeated and repeated again and again until there is what we have called a 'disclosure', until there dawns on us that 'unity', that which can be regarded as the empirical cashing of the word 'continuous'. So with the *Logos*. To talk of eternal procession by no means denies the terms of the sequence. It by no means denies that the *Logos* is now here and now there. But 'eternal' tells such a story about these positionings that there is evoked a disclosure situation, when there dawns on us also a 'sense of unity', a 'kinship', a 'togetherness': everything indeed that we mean by the *Logos* as immanent. So are the two aspects of the *Logos* held together. Just as we have certain functions taking certain particular values, so we have also an immanent *Logos* which also goes forth; and parallel to that connection between the function and its values, of which the word 'continuous' speaks, is the relation between God and Jesus of which the phrase 'eternal procession' speaks. So it is that the 'eternal procession of the *Logos*' expresses in an entirely different logical key, what can be otherwise expressed as the 'eternal generation of the Son'.

However much the two examples stand in need of further development and clarification, it will surely by now be plain that when theologians have sponsored both the model of sonship and the idea of the *Logos* to understand the relationship of God and Jesus, they have been working with two logically different languages. Is not this the point that J. F. Bethune-Baker had in mind in a certain footnote in his *Introduction to the Early History of the Christian Doctrine*? It is a footnote which is far more significant and important than a footnote placing might suggest. In relation to Arius, Bethune-Baker says:

'Arius seems, in part at least, to have been misled by a wrong use of analogy, and by mistaking description for definition. All attempts to explain the nature and relations of the Deity must largely depend on metaphor, and no one metaphor can exhaust those relations. Each metaphor can only describe one aspect of the nature or being of the Deity, and the inferences which can be drawn from it have their limits when they conflict with the inferences which can be truly drawn from other metaphors describing other aspects. From one point of view Sonship is a true description of the inner relations of the Godhead: from another point of view the title *Logos* describes them best. Each metaphor must be limited by the other. The title Son may obviously imply later origin and a distinction amounting to ditheism. It is balanced by the other title *Logos*, which implies co-eternity and inseparable union. Neither title exhausts the relations. Neither may be pressed so far as to exclude the other.'[1]

What Bethune-Baker implies is that at some time or another these relations must be considered, and their logical geography elaborated. It is precisely this work which logical empiricism would do for Christian theology at the present day. Logical empiricism, by its interests and techniques, offers us the possibility of exploring further Bethune-Baker's suggestive and important comments. If we do this, let us realize from the outset however: (a) that if Bethune-Baker is right, Christian doctrine will never give us a blueprint of God. It will talk of God as best it can, but never in terms of more than models, metaphors, key-ideas and the rest; (b) that in particular, the language of Christian doctrine is likely to bristle with improprieties. In surveying Christian doctrine, we must therefore be constantly on the look out for logical oddities, for language that is working oddly. For instance, let us recognize that logical qualifiers are *not* further descriptions, but words which qualify models so as to do justice to what is 'disclosed' in worship. Too often

[1] J. F. Bethune-Baker: *Introduction to the Early History of Christian Doctrine*, Methuen, p. 160.

Christian doctrine has been needlessly confused, and controversies needlessly complicated, by refusing to give qualifiers their correct logical status, supposing them to be somehow descriptive; in which case they would be labels for certain extraordinary features of the theological countryside —describing special sorts of procession, generation and so on. What unedifying and bewildering discussions such mistakes can foster.

These general remarks may be especially illustrated by reference to Nestorianism and Cyril. It will be remembered that the Nestorian controversy in its early days centred largely around the phrase *Theotokos*—'Bearer of God'—or, as it is more popularly translated, 'Mother of God'. We shall leave out of consideration of course the whole historical background of personal intrigue and political manoeuvring; nor need we seek in the least to excuse Anastasius's lack of tact, and his failure to appreciate devotional sentiments. But all that said, there is a sense in which the phrase is logically odd, and if, and in so far as, Anastasius and the Nestorians were making that point, they were performing a useful service. We all know what 'mother of Topsy' means; but 'Mother of God', while similar in grammar, cannot have anything like the same logical structure. $\frac{0}{0}$ may be very similar in appearance to $\frac{2}{3}$, $\frac{3}{4}$, $\frac{21}{67}$, $\frac{1}{2}$, $\frac{1}{13}$, but its logical behaviour is entirely different: hence its appearance in so many mathematical recreations and parlour games.

Now, it may be that orthodoxy failed to realize the logical impropriety of the phrase *Theotokos*; and that is the worst criticism that could be made of it from a philosophical point of view. For, in so far as the orthodox could and might have defended *Theotokos* as a qualified model, justified in worship, they could have made an excellent defence of their position. Further, if the Nestorians had any hunch of logical impropriety it is certainly very unfortunate that they should have spoken as if the impropriety ought to be removed, and that is indeed what they did. But if we remove the impropriety and give *Theotokos* a straightforward logical translation, it can never mean more than that Mary was 'the bearer of one who was to become God', which is what the Nestorians took the phrase to be when they emphasized, and their opponents thought exclusively, our Lord's humanity.

Against this, Cyril talked of 'hypostatic unity' between God and Jesus, but the value of orthodoxy's claim for 'hypostatic' unity must always be proportionate to its refusal to model it. Quite properly, Cyril in his 'Second' or 'dogmatic' Letter of A.D. 430, speaks of hypostatic unity as 'indescribable and inconceivable'. Precisely. The greatest mistake anyone can make is to think that hypostatic union describes some fact in the way that ordinary public languages do. What it essays to talk of is altogether different from observational facts, and its logical functioning is consequentially altogether different as well. So Cyril rightly continues by asserting that 'the Godhead and the manhood, by means of their inexpressible and mysterious concurrence to form a union, have produced for us the one Lord and Son Jesus Christ'. But with regard to this assertion, the first point to notice is that it is cast misleadingly in the material mode. As we read, it sounds like an equation in a sort of psychological chemistry, i.e. Godhead +manhood =Jesus Christ.

Now, what Cyril is saying—or ought to be saying—is something much more complex than this parody would make out, and we may perhaps summarize this more complex claim as follows:

1. For the Early Christians, Jesus Christ was the occasion of and the object of 'disclosure' situations for which normally the word 'God' would have been appropriate currency. Further, much could be said about Jesus Christ which was, on the face of it, straightforwardly empirical, viz. that he was tired, that he wept, and so on. So we have what are *prima facie*, two logically different languages competing as

descriptions of the object of 'disclosure' or 'revelation'. There then arises the problem of how these two languages can somehow be integrated, for in the Christian disclosure *only one* 'object' is disclosed.

2. Hence arises the concept of 'hypostatic' unity, which we may interpret both from a linguistic and a 'factual' point of view.

(i) To know what hypostatic unity is *in fact*, there must be evoked a Christian disclosure situation with Jesus Christ as the occasion and object of it; a situation where we wish to speak of the object as 'Jesus Christ' and yet also as 'God'. This is the *sine qua non* for knowing what hypostatic unity means. There is no alternative way, no easier answer. Further, let us notice that such a Christian disclosure situation can only be evoked; it can never be described, nor can its occurrence be guaranteed by a formula. If we wish to evoke it we may of course use various models with a greater or less chance of success, and if we look at the history of Christian doctrine we may receive certain guidance as to which models are likely to be more helpful. For instance, we shall soon realize that the model of conjunction (συνάφεια) is pretty hopeless as a means of evoking the kind of 'unitary object' for which the phrase 'hypostatic unity' is appropriate. For instance, conjunction might suggest no greater a unity than that of a nut and bolt. No doubt it was this kind of possibility—that it might sponsor such a crude model as this—that led Theodore to prefer 'union' (ἕνωσις) to conjunction, and to give as his model for this 'union' the example of man and wife in marriage. But even this will not guarantee the kind of unitary object which the Christian sees at the heart of his disclosure situation. If then for 'union' we try to picture some even greater unity than that of man and wife in marriage, we might, for instance, hit on the picture of a galloping horseman, which has, I gather, been suggested as the kind of picture which might be fairest at least to

Nestorius, if not to all Nestorians. If we still feel that such a model does not do justice to our unitary object, we shall no doubt move next to the model of a centaur. But then of course our particular model game is up, for while we have now produced a model which is immeasurably better at portraying unity than its predecessors, it is more than likely that it will lead us either to mix the 'natures' (man and horse) or have only one *prosopon* (centaurish appearance) left. In other words, we shall be dangerously near Eutychianism or Nestorianism, and if our game is to have any final moral, it must be that all models are bound sooner or later to show their inadequacy.

We may repeat, that we shall only know what 'hypostatic unity' talks about when there has been evoked for us the Christian disclosure situation. Models may help, and apologetic must see to it that they do help, in such a disclosure, but no model will ever 'explain' or 'describe' that which its use evokes, and which 'hypostatic unity' was coined to deal with.

(ii) As far as *language* goes, what the doctrine of hypostatic unity claims is that to deal with the kind of disclosure situation which is at the basis of Christian revelation, human language must be qualified 'hypostatically', and God language must likewise be qualified 'hypostatically'. Once this has been done, both languages can be used as Christian currency.

So the doctrine of *communicatio idiomatum* becomes the logical claim that two languages of different logical status can nevertheless be used of the one object of the Christian disclosure once they have been suitably qualified, and 'hypostasis' is proffered as a word which is enough of a logical oddity to bring these two languages together and provide a consistent language system for the Christian disclosure. The doctrine of *communicatio idiomatum* and the word 'hypostasis' may both be seen as an ancient attempt to deal with what nowadays would be called the problem of complementary languages and their unity, a problem which is raised especially by recent developments in scientific method.

Let us emphasize that 'hypostasis' would only be successful in unifying two languages if it is odd enough never to be given except by reference to a Christian disclosure situation. If it is to be the logical bond that Christian doctrine wishes it to be, it cannot be modelled. If it is to do this work it is quite impossible (*logically* impossible) to produce a model for it.

If then we agree that 'there is one Person ("hypostasis") and there are two natures' is a concise summary of the orthodox position, we need to be extremely careful about the logical peculiarities of that statement. For what we mean by 'one Person' can never be modelled or described. It can only be given in reference to a Christian disclosure, and for such a situation the only appropriate language is either the language of human nature once it has been suitably qualified to become Christological language; or the language of God when this has been suitably qualified to become Trinitarian language. So when we say that 'there is one Person and there are two natures', what we must always realize is that the 'is' of this statement has a very different logical functioning from the 'are'. The 'is' must have the same logical value as 'hypostasis'; and even the 'are' has two logical values, one relating to assertions about 'human nature', and the other to assertions about 'God'. Small wonder that doctrinal controversies have been bewilderingly complex. They bristle with logical pitfalls.

It is perhaps interesting to give very briefly one further example, that of Patripassianism, as expressed in Tertullian's notable phrase against Praxeas[1]—that he 'crucified the Father'. Patripassianism becomes not an error but an absurdity, a confounding of logical areas, a violation of syntax.

[1] Tertullian: *Adv. Prax.*, 54.

For it uses 'crucify', a word significant only at the Jesus of Nazareth level, of the Father. The truth of Patripassianism is that we cannot say significantly that God suffers. But neither can we significantly say that he does not. Each claim is a misuse of language Yet all this does not imply that suffering cannot be a model which, suitably *qualified*, is currency for God.

As we survey the developments of Christology and Trinitarian doctrine, what is evident, however, is how often the heretics run some model or other—sometimes a highly sophisticated model—to death, in a passionate desire to understand. Opponents then come forward with other models which show the inadequacy of the first, but they too develop them beyond necessity, and court fresh heresies at the next move. But let us not be made sceptical by such shuttlecock theology. Let us rather recall what we said in relation to the Bethune-Baker footnote.[1] The shuttlecock character of the early history of Christian doctrine only arises because the ball could never be left to rest in any one empirical court. The struggle to understand God can never come to a satisfactory end; the language game can never be completed. Broadly speaking, what orthodoxy did was to support the winner of every heat. Orthodoxy aimed at having every possible model, and it pressed each model into such service as it could give. To press any model was sure, however, to make evident sooner or later, its inadequacy. So we can see why the orthodoxy of one century became so near to being the heresy of the next. But in the end, and most necessary of all, orthodoxy sponsored a word such as 'hypostasis' which, resistent to any or all modelling, would be sure to preserve the mystery. So theology spends every philosophical model and more. It must necessarily in this sense exhibit always a Chalcedonian bankruptcy: like many other people's banking accounts at the present time, it will

[1] See pp. 163-4 above.

only show an active healthy condition when its store of empirical models is overdrawn. For it has invisible assets— mystery—of which the models take no account.

Christian doctrine does not give a picture of God in the sense of a verbal photograph. Christian doctrine can only be justified on an epistemology very different from that which lay behind traditional views of metaphysics. In no sense is Christian doctrine a 'super-science'. Its structure, and its anchorage in 'fact' are much more complex than that parallel would suggest. What we have been trying to do in these various examples has been to give hints—no more—of how traditional Christian phrases might otherwise be elucidated and justified. If they are anchored in 'disclosure' situations, situations which centre directly or indirectly on Jesus of Nazareth and are in part mysterious and elusive, only then can Christian phrases be given a logical complexity suited to their theme. An empirical approach to philosophical theology takes the traditional phrases of Christian doctrine and sees in this way what logical placing they must have to tell their tale; being sure of only one thing, that an adequate account of their logical structure will never be given on an ordinary view of 'facts' accompanied by the idea that language provides a sort of verbal photograph which is in a one-one correspondence to what it talks about. To make such a mistake would be to confound the logic of theology with that of some precision language such as those of which the sciences make use.

The point above any other that I would like to emphasize is, then, the logical complexity of doctrinal assertions. So, how barren and verbal are those doctrinal controversies where each side supposes they are using straightforward homogeneous language, and talking in the material mode; whereas in point of fact they are only each sponsoring different models in order to understand, as best they can, a mystery which is bound to exceed both their attempts. So we sympathize with Augustine's view that doctrine only 'fences a mystery'; and we express ourselves doctrinally only because we cannot live and keep silent.

After these various examples and general reflections, let us broaden our story yet further by recognizing that there will be at least three logical areas in Christian doctrine corresponding to the terms which occur in that outline of the Christian claim which we formulated above:[1] 'God did something through Jesus.' The claim which these words express, may be developed in at least three ways, according as to whether it seeks an expression in terms of some appropriate subject word only, some appropriate object word only, or some appropriate relational word only. The Christian claim may be expressed, for example, by having some symbol more complex than 'God'; or by having a symbol which talks of 'what God did' in Jesus; or it may concentrate on some object-symbol in whose occurrence such activity is manifestly displayed. There are thus at least three cases, and we will look at each in turn:

(i) In the first case, the Christian claim may lead (as we have seen) to the construction of a revised key word for our language, a variant for 'God'. 'God' (we might say) needs to be given a 'hypostatic' qualification to become full Christian currency. There will thus arise a 'Trinitarian formula' instead of the 'God' of natural theology, and various phrases in the traditional Creeds can then be seen as giving logical rules for the construction and use of such a revised apex word.

(ii) Alternatively, Christian doctrine might attempt to explicate its claim in terms of some relational word, e.g. 'justification'; 'redemption'; and so on.

(iii) Thirdly, the claim may be expressed in terms of object words such as 'Church,' 'Episcopacy', 'Sacraments', about whose logical settings it is very important to be clear

[1] See p. 155.

if unnecessary misunderstandings, or confused claims are to be avoided.

It is plain that reckoning with no more than these three logically distinguishable areas in Christian doctrine, there arise already many possibilities of logical blunders and cross-purpose talking. More positively, what I hope to do by discussing each area quite briefly, is to show the importance of logical mapping as a preliminary to Christian controversy or doctrinal discussion. It can certainly help us to avoid many unnecessary misunderstandings and pointless arguments.

(i) *First of all, then, let us consider the expression of the Christian Claim in terms of a revised formula for 'God'.*

The early Christians came to realize that the discernment-commitment which led them, as Jews, to speak of 'God', was not only one which was occasioned by Jesus as well, whom they thus came to speak of as the 'Son of God'; it was also known in the Upper Room and at Pentecost, when it was talked of also in terms of the 'Holy Spirit'. The leading question was: Could Christians talk like this, yet consistently? Could 'God', 'Jesus' and 'Holy Spirit' be used more or less interchangeably? In what we have called the first area of Christian doctrine, its early history was essentially an endeavour to deal with this problem of consistent talking. The early Christological and Trinitarian controversies are wrongly seen if they are thought to be concerned with super-scientific discoveries about God, as though the Early Fathers had some special high-powered telescope by which to inspect the God-head; or as though they had discovered, for the benefit of posterity, that to ring CHAlcedon 451 would invariably give us an up-to-date report on heavenly events. What the early controversies settled were rather rules for our talking, and what came out of them at the end were new symbols for our use, and in particular the Trinitarian formula. The Christian does not have the single word 'God' as his key word. He substitutes for that symbol another; and this other symbol is built out from that focus of our total commitment which is made up of the elements of the Christian dispensation. It is a symbol which (as we have seen) qualifies God hypostatically. Let us look somewhat more closely at its logical structure.

The Christian says in effect—for 'God' read

$$\begin{matrix} & \text{Father} & \\ \diagup & & \diagdown \\ \text{Son} & \text{—} & \text{Holy Spirit.} \end{matrix}$$

Now, if the logical move puzzles us may I suggest that we can profitably reflect on the logical changes there were when the compact benzene formula C_6H_6 became

the ring formula

$$\begin{matrix} & \text{CH} & \\ \diagup & & \diagdown \\ \text{HC} & & \text{CH} \\ | & & | \\ \text{HC} & & \text{CH} \\ \diagdown & & \diagup \\ & \text{CH} & \end{matrix}$$

Or, to use the benzene example for rather a different purpose, we might profitably call to mind the doctrine of chemical 'resonance'. For various experimental reasons, organic chemists have begun to speak of *two* varieties of the benzene ring formula we have given above, instead of only one, and between these two, they speak of 'resonance', where this is used as a unifying word between different formulae he used about what was once called simply 'benzene'. In this way, we might say that 'resonance' plays a logical part somewhat similar to that which 'hypostasis' plays in theology, where 'hypostasis' is a unifying word between different phrases, each talking of what hitherto was called simply 'God'. Not that the two cases are anything like identical; but if the theological change seems quite strange and abstruse these two examples from organic chemistry may not be without their usefulness.

At any rate, to return to our theme, the Athanasian Creed may be seen for the most part as a set of logical rules for constructing the Trinitarian formula. For it expresses the symmetry of the Trinitarian symbol by first qualifying certain models each in the same way, *and then insisting* that they may all replace the same word 'God'. (a) For example, the Creed speaks of 'the Father uncreate, the Son uncreate: and the Holy Ghost uncreate. The Father incomprehensible, the Son incomprehensible: and the Holy Ghost incomprehensible. The Father eternal, the Son eternal: and the Holy Ghost eternal.' Here are three groups of identically qualified models, and after our various illustrations in Chapter II, we need perhaps here develop only one more example: e.g. Father, uncreate, incomprehensible, eternal.

'Father' is now the model; a word we know specifying situations with which we are familiar. If we have had a good home, already some picture is before our minds: the father's hand guiding and helping the child who holds it; the father as a symbol of concern for the child and of the child's dependence on him. On the other hand, human fathers are limited; all of us quiver before our sons' headmasters; and the time comes when a son knows all that his father does and a bit more; when the son *comprehends* his father through and through. Even more seriously, fathers are *creatures* themselves, with their own frailties, and in due *time* they die. So if we are to use father-situations at all we must somehow group them to tell the right kind of stories. Here is one part of the significance of words like 'incomprehensible', 'uncreate', 'eternal'. These are stimulants to move us in the right direction along a series of father-situations. They are directives so that we shall think away the inappropriate features. If by assimilating Father Almighty to Father Christmas we have grown accustomed to thinking of God with a beard, here is a directive that we should shave it off. So these words like 'uncreate, incomprehensible, eternal', tell us *how to develop* pictures of fatherhood, and the stories would extend to the father of the Prodigal Son and his brother, and to our

175

Lord's own use of the fatherhood model. The stories would extend indeed until there broke in on us that challenge in whose acceptance is a full commitment of the kind we were describing in earlier chapters.

Nor is that all; and here is again the second significance of words like uncreate. The story having been told till this commitment was evoked, words like 'incomprehensible', 'uncreate', 'eternal', have then, as we saw, another function, which comes from the very puzzlement which it creates for the phrase in which it stands. How can a father—it might be said—be almighty, incómprehensible, eternal? But this very puzzle, scandal, or impropriety, shows us that the word for which the phrase stands, i.e. 'God', has a placing away from all 'father' language. It is indeed a key word for all language. In this sense 'uncreate' and its logical kinsmen are signposts to the odd logical placing of our key word 'God'. Words like 'uncreate' are therefore both stimulants and signposts; they are what we have called *logical qualifiers*. Once again we notice how different, and how *necessarily* different the phrase 'Father uncreate' is from other phrases, which while similar in grammar to it, have an altogether different logic, e.g. Father Christmas, Father Superior. Once again let not puzzlements arise because we allocate the phrase wrongly; because we file it into the wrong logical folder: as though we were to assimilate Cowley Father to Heavenly Father, and then ask whether or not Heaven is like Cowley.

In this way, then, we may interpret such phrases as the 'Father uncreate . . . incomprehensible . . . eternal' from the Athanasian Creed, and notice in passing how logical misunderstandings may lead many people to suppose the phrases are sheer rubbish. We all know the tale of the choirman singing lustily 'the Father incomprehensible . . . ' and *sotto voce* saying to his neighbour 'the whole thing incomprehensible'. I hope I have suggested ways of eliminating such misunderstandings as that.

(b) Here, then, are various qualified models. The Creed now continues: 'And yet they are not three eternals: but one eternal . . . *there is but one God.*' In other words, the Creed pleads the logical symmetry of a group formula about a point 'God' from which each model is distant by the same qualifiers, and the whole replacing the 'God' of natural theology:

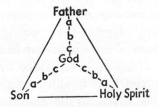

(a =uncreate, b =incomprehensible, c =eternal)

But, you may say, what of a key *word* if our key symbol has a number of terms? There is certainly need to assert some kind of logical priority amongst the terms. Hence such a phrase as 'proceeding from the Father and the Son', which in its linguistic aspect, begins to specify the structure of the key symbol and claims (we would suggest) *logical* priority for Father and Son. Further, Christian theology would wish to claim—what the *Filioque* clause somewhat conceals— logical priority of Father over Son. Gregory Nazianzus in his *Orations*, e.g., had claimed that the Father was 'ἄναρχος' (unoriginate); that is, we would say, logically prior to all. Hence the logical relation is expressed more appropriately in temporal prepositions 'ἐκ' and 'διά'—proceeding *from*

the Father *through* the Son:
$$\begin{array}{c} \text{Father} \\ \swarrow \quad \searrow \\ \text{Son} \rightarrow \text{Holy Spirit.} \end{array}$$
The result

is that our group symbol has one term—'Father'—with the needed logical priority.

One last point, since we have been concerned with the

Athanasian Creed and possible misunderstandings due to logical misallocations.

Let us recall the notorious difficulties about verse 2: 'which Faith except everyone do keep whole and undefiled: without doubt he shall perish everlastingly'. But whenever we stumble on such difficulties let our first reaction be: Have I given the phrase the appropriate logical structure? Have I rightly allocated it? Now I suggest that the verse is *not* saying: 'Swallow this or die,' 'Insure or perish'—securing conviction by threat. Rather is its logical structure to be understood as follows. The *Quicunque vult* as a whole expresses the commitment alternatively described by the phrase 'life eternal'—another model and qualifier. Without this commitment, without this Creed as its guarantor, no one has 'eternal life'. The Creed is thus logically synonymous with 'life eternal'. So, to specify its rejection, alternatives must be formulated whose logical placing is equivalent to that of '*no* life eternal'. Thus we may have, for example, '*damnation* eternal', '*fire* everlasting', or '*perish* everlasting(ly)', where it is plain that the words 'damnation', 'fire' and 'perish' are *models* meant to tell the same tale as '*no life*'. To perish is to lose life; fire destroys life, and damnation or judgment at least compromise it. The logical placing of 'eternal damnation', 'everlasting fire', and 'perish everlastingly' is as complex as this. Here are phrases meant to evoke that state which accompanies a positive rejection of the Christian claim: models of such a kind that the qualifiers work so as to evoke (if they succeed) infidelity. 'Hell fire'; and 'everlasting fire' have a logical behaviour as complex as that. So we must not confuse coal fire and continuous burning fire, with hell fire. To start drawing plans of the great Assize Court or asking scientific questions about the temperatures of hell fire, is to make a logical blunder—to suppose grammatical similarity means logical kinship.

But to summarize our main point: What the Athanasian

Creed does in particular is to commend as the Christian key word a new symbol for 'God'. It formulates rules for its construction; it gives the symbol an appropriate logical structure. For the most part the Creed is thus purely formal, and needs for its understanding and content the Christian disclosure which, at best, would be otherwise given in that worshipful situation where the Creed naturally occurs.

So much for attempts to express the Christian claim by varying the symbol 'God'.

(ii) *Let us now see how the Christian claim has sometimes been expressed in terms of a relational word, which however must then have a suitably odd logical status.*

In an endeavour to evoke and express the whole Christian situation, Christians have used words like, for instance, 'justification' or 'redemption' which may be regarded as descriptive of a 2 (or a 3) term relation—God-Jesus on the one hand, the Christian on the other. But it has then been LXX 'δικαιοσύνη' with a difference; it has been the Red Sea LXX 'ἀπολύτρωσις' with a difference; and New Testament theologians have been keenest of anyone to point this out. C. H. Dodd, for example, has emphasized how, to express the Christian gospel, Paul claims that God 'justifies' the sinful, *despite* the explicit condemnation of any such 'justification' of the sinful which occurs in Proverbs 17.15: 'He that justifieth the wicked . . . (is) an abomination to the Lord.' In this way, Dodd explains, St Paul ensures that Christian 'justification' is seen as something which breaks through the logic of Torah legalism. 'Justification', as used in the New Testament, must differ from justification in the Old Testament as much as the Trinitarian formula differs from 'God'.

But for our present purpose we may concentrate on just two points which emphasize and illustrate the fact that when relational words descriptive of some sort of activity are used to epitomize the gospel, they must be given an appropriate logical status.

(1) When relational words such as 'Justification' or 'Satisfaction' or 'Redemption' have been made currency for the whole Christian situation, they have often been then given the status of key words. So, for some, 'justification' has had well-nigh the logical placing of 'God'—the same kind of placing that many materialistic physicists gave to 'atom', or biologists to 'evolution' in the nineteenth century. 'Justification' has been something for which people have been ready to die, and many of the reformers did. This is precisely what our logical considerations would lead us to expect. Further, it is interesting to notice that whereas it has been the first logical area of Christian doctrine which has most appealed to theologians and philosophers, it has been this second area, which is fixed on relational words, which has most often appealed to preachers and reformers. This only underlines on the one hand the gap there often seems between the Trinitarian formula and the gospel situation, the 'good news' it is meant to talk about—a gap I hope I have done a little to bridge; yet, on the other hand, how necessary it is that a 'Triune God' and not 'Justification' should be given the key place in any Christian theological language. A theology which cannot be preached is about as objectionable as preaching which cannot be theologically defended.

(2) Another point: some have been tempted to read words such as 'justification' as though they belonged to the language of morality. For instance, it has sometimes been supposed that the Christian who claims to have been 'justified', 'redeemed' and 'sanctified', is expressing a claim which relates directly to his observable behaviour—that 'being justified' is a logical synonym for 'being good'. But when these words of Christian doctrine have been given such an ethical placing, people then remark (and rightly) that since

no Christian is wholly 'good', either there are no Christians, no one has been 'justified', or Christian doctrine is plainly false. But the truth is that the dilemma arises out of the over-simple logical assimilation with which the argument began. 'Justification' and 'doing wrong' are not logical synonyms, belonging to the same logical area, and we cannot link them directly in a significant question. 'Can we do wrong after justification?' is not at all like 'Can we contract diphtheria after inoculation?' It is not even like 'Will his behaviour be more predictable after such and such a brain operation has been performed?' That some sort of connection can be discovered on the theistic map between 'justification' and moral behaviour is undeniable. But it is of a most complex kind, which makes the question: 'Can we do wrong after justification?' just as improper and misleading as the question: 'Can we contract diphtheria after baptism?' We need not deny that what 'justification' talks about will have some sort of connection with moral behaviour; we need not deny that since 'baptism' concerns the 'whole man', it will have some sort of connection with health; but what is characteristic and distinctive about 'justification' and 'baptism' belongs to different logical areas altogether. 'Being justified' and 'being good' are no more logically interchangeable than 'being baptized' and 'being cured'. If and when 'justification' expresses the characteristically Christian claim, such a question as: 'Can we do wrong after justification?' will be logically skew, and any discussion of it is bound to lead to crooked answers. This is the reflection we might make after reading St Paul's discussion on post-baptismal sin.[1] What we have to realize is that if the Christian message *is* talked of in terms of such relational words, they will never be straightforwardly translated into (for instance) ethical concepts relating to observable behaviour. There will always be a logical gap between 'grace' and the 'graces'. Ethical

[1] Rom. 6.

words can never be more than models in relation to distinctive Christian situations.

> (iii) *Finally, what of the third logical area of Christian doctrine which attempts to talk of the Christian claim in terms of object words such as 'church', 'episcopacy', 'sacraments'?*

Once again I will do no more than emphasize on the one hand that, when such words become adequate currency for the full Christian claim, their logical status must be appropriately odd. As key words for language there then go together, as suitable kinsmen: 'Church' and 'Body of Christ'; 'Episcopacy' and 'Apostolic succession'; 'Sacraments' and 'Real Presence'. In each case, the second member of the pair makes it quite explicit that the earlier words are to be given a Trinitarian status. With such a placing they become also logical kinsmen with 'justification' as the Reformers used it. Once again we have words which people—though not often the same people—have thought it right to die for.

But it is important to realize, on the other hand, that an altogether different logical status might be, and often is, given to words such as 'church', 'episcopacy'. and 'sacraments'. These might be no more than object-words in a straightforward empirical sense, when 'Church' =clergy and people; and very much a *corpus permixtum;* when 'Episcopacy' =the bench of bishops; and 'the Sacraments' =bread and wine for a memorial meal. Here are words with a straightforward observational logic, and to enhance their status so that they become unmistakable currency for the full Christian claim, we have to tell around them the kind of story by means of which a Christian disclosure will be evoked. For instance, we may start with 'Episcopacy' as 'this bishop and that', but from such a beginning, and if we developed an appropriate theological story, we might arrive at 'Episcopacy' as a Christian key word anchored in the full Christian disclosure. This would then be 'Episcopacy', which, like God himself, is according to Cyprian 'one' (*episcopatus unus est*), something which is significantly linked with what is called the 'unity' of the Church. Here is a logically homogeneous network, but the status of 'Church' is that of 'Episcopacy' in its more-than-empirical sense.

All I wish to do here, is to show how very necessary it is to distinguish these two logical areas, and we may give two illustrations—the one from Richard Hooker, and the other from Lancelot Andrewes—to illustrate the point.

(i) Hooker may have been very judicious, but I think that his claim that 'episcopacy' was of the *bene esse* but not of the *esse* of the Church, not only fails to recognize that 'Episcopacy' may behave in two logically different ways, but does not notice at all that particular kind of logical behaviour which is, and most appropriately, odd.

That which some claim is of the *esse* of the Church is (we may say) 'Episcopacy' with a capital E, such a word as is a kinsman of 'God', one whose logical placing is as complex as that. Here we have what might be called theological Episcopacy. On the other hand, that which others claim is of the *bene esse* of the Church—what we may call 'small e' episcopacy or empirical episcopacy—is episcopacy known in terms of prelacy, bishops, stipends, reunion schemes, Church Commissioners and the rest. Here (we might say) is observable episcopacy. But these are two logical areas, which will only be bridged when stories about the latter can be so developed as to evoke a specifically Christian disclosure in relation to which alone theological Episcopacy can be commended. In this connection we can see the importance of a recent book which claims that Episcopacy is of the *plene esse* of the Church.[1] For we may say that such a view (a) recognizes implicitly, if not explicitly, the double logical status of 'episcopacy', and (b) tries to unite these two logical

[1] Ed. K. M. Carey: *The Historic Episcopate.*

values by means of the model of 'filling' developed within a historical background.

(ii) For the second example let us give credit to Lancelot Andrewes that he had the devotional and logical insight to see that the phrase 'Real Presence' is odd, and not to be 'explained' in any system of public language. All we can do to understand it (he said in effect) is to parallel it with other equally odd phrases, in the hope that a Christian disclosure situation will be evoked. We can do no better than to quote Andrewes' own words in his *Response to the Apologia of Cardinal Bellarmine:* 'We believe no less than you (Cardinal Bellarmine), that the presence is real. (But) Concerning the *method* of the presence, we define nothing rashly, and, I add, we do not anxiously enquire, any more than *how* the blood of Christ washes us in our baptism, any more than *how* the human and divine natures are united in one person in the incarnation of Christ . . .' (italics mine). In other words, Andrewes takes the laudable empirical line that if we want to know what 'Real Presence' is, all we can say is that 'Christ' or the 'Son of God' is present in the Sacraments, *as* he is present in Jesus of Nazareth, *as* he is present in Baptism, *and so on,*—hoping that the 'penny will drop'—and Anglicans take this same line when they associate didactically the Eucharist with the fellowship of worshippers constituting the Church as Christ's Body, and insist that there shall be no Celebration without a 'convenient number'. For the 'presence' of Christ in the Sacraments on the one hand, is to be portrayed and equated with, it is logically interchangeable with, the 'presence' of Christ in the Church on the other. It is true that these didactic considerations, which have always been a strong feature of Anglicanism, may lead to an over-restricted view of Eucharistic doctrine, but we cannot doubt that as far as it goes at any rate, traditional Anglican teaching is inspired by a sound empirical insight.

What now at the end? A final reflection: How important

logical empiricism can be for theological analysis, and in particular how it can help us to clarify Christian controversies by elucidating the logical placings of traditional Christian phrases. But make no mistake, I do not claim that here is something altogether new. We might well admit that in principle we are only doing what, for example, St Thomas Aquinas was doing, though we are not thereby committed (for better or worse) to his ontology and system. We may perhaps say that logical empiricism offers us a possible *generalization* of Thomism for bringing new life to old and complex controversies; by helping us defend those logical improprieties that are so often a stumbling block to our pastoral ministries. Best of all, logical empiricism can start and end by recognizing its limitations—that it is grappling with a mystery that even logical improprieties can only do their best to portray or evoke.

If the reader thinks that logical empiricism will have a tendency to make theology 'verbal', he is right if he means by this that it would invent no 'entities' beyond necessity. But at the same time I would emphasize that in the end the one 'factual' reference it preserves is the one which alone matters, the one which is given in worship. God and his worship: logical empiricism, put to the service of theology, starts and ends there. Need we trouble if we discover meanwhile that a whole heap of metaphysical furniture—underlying 'substances', 'indelible characteristics', and so on—which some might have supposed to be indispensable, has in fact belonged only to a confusing dream?

I hope I have made it plain, then, that in theology we talk about a situation which, from the point of view of 'what is seen', is empirically odd; a situation known best perhaps in what can be called compactly 'worship'; a situation which is one of 'discernment' and 'commitment'. If theology is to do justice to such a situation it must exhibit an appropriately odd logical structure. The duty which has always been laid, and will ever be laid, on the Christian apologist, is to formulate such logical allocations of traditional phrases as do justice to both the churchmen of the past and our own cirumstances in the present.

Finally, if we misunderstand the logical structure of a theological phrase, we can be guilty of the most absurd mistakes. Indeed, the very fun poked at theology, measures often the logical blunder which has been committed; as the joke cracked by the school cleaner—regretting that children still haven't found that Least Common Multiple after so many years of searching—is a measure of her misreading of mathematics.

Not the least merit of logical empiricism, then, is that it provides us with an inroad into theology which can break down misunderstandings, and by centering attention on to both language and 'facts', can from the beginning hope to be both intellectually honest and devotionally helpful—a combination not always achieved.

INDEX OF NAMES

GENERAL INDEX

INDEX OF BIBLICAL REFERENCES